CAREERS IN
MEDICINE

By
CAROLYN SIMPSON
and PENELOPE HALL, M.D.

D0101410

The Rosen Publishing Group, Inc.
NEW YORK

Published in 1994 by The Rosen Publishing Group, Inc.
29 East 21st Street, New York, NY 10010

First Edition

Simpson, Carolyn.
    Careers in medicine / by Carolyn Simpson and Penelope Hall. —
1st ed.
    Includes bibliographical references and index.
    ISBN 0-8239-1711-8 ISBN 0-8239-1712-6 (pbk)
    1. Medicine—Vocational guidance—Juvenile literature. [1.
Physicians. 2. Occupations. 3. Medicine—Vocational guidance. 4.
Vocational guidance.] I. Hall, Penelope, M.D.
    R690.S53 1993
    610.69—dc20   93-28011
                                                        CIP
                                                         AC

Manufactured in the United States of America

About the Authors

Carolyn Simpson has worked in the mental health field for the past twenty years, primarily as a clinical social worker and educator. She received a Bachelor's Degree in Sociology from Colby College, Waterville, Maine, and a Master's Degree in Human Relations from the University of Oklahoma, Norman.

She is the author of several books, including *Coping with Teenage Motherhood*, *Coping with An Unplanned Pregnancy*, *Coping with Emotional Problems*, and *Careers in Social Work*—the last two coauthored with her husband, Dwain Simpson. She currently teaches Psychology at Tulsa Junior College.

For this book, she teamed up with her childhood buddy, Penelope Hall. Both women grew up in Augusta, Maine, graduating from Cony High School in 1969. Their last joint effort was a science project on amoebas, back in 1965. . . .

Penelope Hall is a board-certified internist, specializing in geriatric medicine, in private practice in Billerica, Massachusetts. She received a Bachelor's Degree from Bates College, Lewiston, Maine, and a medical degree from the University of Vermont Medical School. She spent three years of residency training in internal medicine at Worcester Memorial Hospital in Worcester, Massachusetts, and two additional years there in a geriatric fellowship. She later completed a one-year geriatric research fellowship at the Bedford Veterans Center in Bedford, Massachusetts.

Dr. Hall has lived and worked in Georgia, California, and Okinawa as well as her native New England. In her spare time, she paints (mostly watercolors)—a passion left over from childhood.

Acknowledgments

Special thanks to Sallie Clote of Norman, Oklahoma, for her help in gathering some of the data for this book.

Thanks, too, to all the physicians who responded to my questionnaire, taking time out of their busy schedules to reflect upon their profession.

And most of all: thank you Dwain, Michal, Jaime, and Jarrett for "not minding so much" when I shut myself up in my room to put this book together. I promise you all a **real meal** soon!

C.S.
March, 1993

Table of Contents

Foreword

CHOOSING TO BECOME A DOCTOR

Becoming a doctor is not the easiest job in the world. In fact, it is a long and difficult road, and many a student has dropped out of the running along the way. In the first place, merely getting into medical school is an ordeal, and staying on top of the workload once you're there is equally challenging. The competition for desired positions, the demanding hours, and lack of sleep continue throughout the next three to four years of residency training. For many physicians, the more you study, the more you realize you can never know enough. And though the scutwork decreases as you rise through the ranks of your program, the responsibilities increase. At long last, you see the light at the end of the tunnel! You've survived your residency and are now ready to start working (and being regarded) as a real live doctor. Especially getting paid as one! The only problem: You're going to have to earn a whole heck of a lot of money because you've got $100,000 worth of medical school loans to repay, starting that very month . . .

When most people picture doctors, they think of men (and occasionally women) making huge sums of money, driving new BMWs or Mercedes, and traveling to sunbaked islands during winter. Of course, some doctors are able to do those very things, but if you're interested in becoming a doctor only for the wealth and status, let me assure you there are easier ways to get them. True, doctors as a rule are well compensated and enjoy the respect of their community, but everything has its price. The tradeoffs for financial security and prestige are the demanding work schedules that continue long after residency training ends, and the stress that accompanies patient care. Given the number of hours needed to sustain a practice, one really doesn't go into medicine solely for the money.

So why become a doctor, then? Good doctors will tell you they do so for two reasons: a genuine desire to help people—to make a difference in someone's life—and the sheer challenge. Finding the cause of a disease, finding the right treatment once diagnosis has been made, and even better, finding a cure make this career all worth it. One doctor who answered my questionnaire detailed all the horrors of medical school and the grueling hours in his residency program (during which his marriage fell apart). And yet, asked if he would go through it all again just to be a doctor, he replied, "You bet! In a minute!"

PART ONE

UNDERSTANDING THE MEDICAL PROFESSION

1

A History of Healers and Modern Doctors

The early healer-priests called shamans served as doctors to their tribes. Lacking any scientific knowledge of disease or cures, they relied on the practice of "white magic": the use of rituals, seances, and hallucinogenic drugs to drive out bad spirits. Later shamans used herbs, including the bark of certain trees, to treat pain and illness. Many drugs used today are based on these plant extracts. Aspirin, derived from the bark of the willow and meadowsweet was a popular folk remedy for fever and pain. Native Americans and some Eastern cultures continued to rely on shamans and what has come to be called "alternative medicine" well into the modern age.

THE ANCIENTS
The practice of medicine became more scientific under the influence of Western thought. Hippocrates of Greece, in the fifth century B.C., taught that medicine is an art and that it is the doctor's responsibility "to help, or at least to do no harm." He is credited with having written the Hippocratic Oath, which all doctors take today upon graduation from medical school. Hippoc-

rates, called "the father of medicine," expected doctors to possess the highest principles so as not to dishonor the medical profession. Although he erred in his assumption that disease resulted from an imbalance in the four bodily humors, he introduced the idea of scientific observation for purposes of diagnosis. He also had said it was the physician's responsibility to provide the right circumstances (suggest to the patient a better diet, fresh air, exercise) for healing to take place.

Galen was another Greek physician, of second-century Greece, remembered for his use of healing plants. Being trained in surgical techniques, he got himself appointed surgeon to care for the gladiators in Rome's Coliseum. Galen, an arrogant man, demonstrated the confidence (some say "conceit") that was so necessary to the prosperous physician of the day. Although he wrote and lectured extensively about the body's functions, he reportedly never based any information on human dissection. Relying on animal dissection obviously led to many inaccuracies (later uncovered by the French anatomist Andreas Vesalius, 1514–64). He did recognize, however, that the brain, not the heart, was responsible for thinking; and he encouraged other doctors to verify things with their own eyes—not to accept unquestioned everything they read in books. Galen's beliefs, as well as his inaccuracies, stood for centuries.

ADVENT OF CHRISTIANITY

With the establishment of Christianity as Europe's official religion, secular medicine was essentially discarded. In medieval Europe, the Christian clergy did all the healing. Because sickness and disease were viewed as the devil's work, treatment often included praying over the patient, performing ritual exorcisms, chanting, and having the patient touch holy relics. People also believed that God intended mortals to suffer when they were ill, so no significant effort was made to assuage pain.

Much of Galen's works was garbled in the many translations it underwent. Unfortunately, the inaccuracies coupled with the actual errors in translation persisted for centuries.

In medieval Europe, surgery was performed (for life-threatening conditions) by "barber-surgeons." They were not university-educated, as were the physicians. They learned their trade in apprenticeship to other barber-surgeons, and despite their skill, they were never accorded the status of physicians. This division of labor and difference in stature continued well into the sixteenth century.

Andreas Vesalius, at the age of twenty-eight, wrote the first accurate book of anatomy in 1543. Besides being far more accurate, *De Humani Corporis Fabrica* contained beautiful illustrations. Leonardo Da Vinci himself studied at the dissecting tables of anatomists. Unlike Galen, Vesalius used human bodies for dissection and thus was able to correct many of Galen's misperceptions. Anatomists used bodies of executed criminals for their first dissections. Professors of anatomy lectured about the parts and functions of the body, while barber-surgeons dissected. When Vesalius became a professor, he combined the roles: lecturing, demonstrating, and dissecting. In all, he identified 200 inaccuracies in Galen's works.

INTRODUCTION OF SCIENCE

As we have said, sixteenth-century barber-surgeons were mere tradesmen. Ambroise Paré (1517?–1590), a French barber-surgeon, changed all that. As surgeon to the king, Paré helped improve the barber-surgeons' standing in society. Besides elevating their status, he made two other important contributions to medicine.

5

Being assigned to the military legions, he mostly dealt with battle wounds. At those times, physicians poured boiling oil into wounds to encourage healing. On one occasion, Paré ran out of oil and used a concoction of egg yolk, rose oil, and turpentine to dress the wound. Naturally, soldiers preferred the soothing lotion, and much to the physicians' surprise, the wounds dressed with Paré's concoction healed as well as those dressed in the standard way. Paré ushered in a new concept: gentleness in the treatment of wounds. In addition, Paré learned to tie off blood vessels during amputations, which made the procedure far more successful.

Until the nineteenth century, physicians used a method of thumping the chest and listening to the different sounds it produced to determine the status of the organs inside. This was the method René Laënnec (1781–1826) had used until one day in 1816 a well-endowed woman patient needed a diagnosis. Too embarrassed to lay his ear against her breast, Laënnec rolled a wad of papers he was carrying into a cylinder and put one end against the woman's chest and the other end to his ear. He was surprised to discover how much the cylinder improved the sounds he was attempting to hear. That hurriedly put-together roll of papers constituted the first stethoscope. Laënnec later perfected the instrument, which was so vital in magnifying the sounds of infection and disease.

WOMEN ENTER THE SCENE

In 1847, in the United States, Elizabeth Blackwell (1821–1910) became the first woman admitted to medical school. The student body of Geneva College in upstate New York voted (actually as a joke) to accept her into their medical school; she had already been turned down by 29 others. Many doctors who were impressed with her skill and commitment suggested she masquer-

6

ade as a man in order to get her medical education. Ms. Blackwell refused, preferring to challenge the assumption that only men could be doctors.

At this time, American medical education consisted of several years of private study and only two years of formal medical school. A person preparing to be a doctor need never work with an actual patient until after graduation. Elizabeth Blackwell graduated from medical school in 1849 but still found herself facing a brick wall. Hospitals would not grant her privileges to practice, and most people (women included) were reluctant to trust a woman who aspired to a "man's" profession. Ms. Blackwell went to Europe to train in the only area allowed a woman in those days: midwifery. Eventually she returned to America. Together they opened a clinic for the poor. In 1868, after years of struggle, they opened the Women's Medical College of the New York Infirmary, with stiffer entrance requirements than any medical school at the time. Instead of the customary ten months of classroom training, this school required three years, and courses were graded. Students were also expected to work with actual patients. Elizabeth Blackwell faced a lifetime of resistance not only to her ideas, but also to her presence. Nonetheless, because of her persistence, women today are able to enter fields undreamed of a short hundred years ago.

A CENTURY OF DISCOVERIES

Many consider the Civil War to be the last war fought in "the medical dark ages." Even though physicians knew about anesthesia as early as 1846, anesthetics were not generally available to army doctors, and the vast majority of amputations were performed without them. Small wonder that soldiers faced with battlefield amputation prayed to die. Also, the existence of germs was not known; more people died from infections introduced during surgery than from the surgery itself.

The discovery of nitrous oxide (laughing gas) and ether ended the centuries of pain people had endured in order to "get better." Humphry Davy (1778–1829), who was British, first discussed the effects of nitrous oxide in 1798. People held "laughing gas" parties and "ether" parties (after Michael Faraday (1791–1867) had discovered the effects of that anesthetic). After attending one of these parties, Dr. Crawford W. Long (1815–1878) decided to operate on a patient using ether as an anesthetic. In 1842 he successfully removed a cyst from a patient's neck. Breathing into a towel soaked in ether, the patient remained pain-free throughout the operation. Unfortunately for Long, who did not publish his results until seven years later, he failed to gain credit for being first to use ether as an anesthetic.

In 1844–45 Horace Wells (1815–1848), a dentist in Hartford, Connecticut, started using nitrous oxide in his practice. His student, William Thomas Green Morton (1819–1868), who practiced in Boston, experimented with ether. In 1846 he persuaded a surgeon to let him anesthetize a patient before an audience. The operation was not only a success, but pain-free, thanks to Morton's anesthesia.

Surgery may have been pain-free by 1850, but it was no less risky. Patients still died as often as not from infections incurred during surgery. An English surgeon, Joseph Lister (1827–1912), concluded that something must be getting into the wound to cause the infection. Having read about Louis Pasteur's discovery that any liquid boiled would remain "germ-free" as long as it was covered, he determined that it must be "germ-laden dust particles" in the air that were infecting the wounds.

Although Lister had the right idea—that germs from

outside the wound were causing the infections—he came up with some curious solutions to the problem. He first used carbolic acid to cleanse and treat the wounds. He sprayed special chemicals into the air around the operating table to disinfect the dust. In 1867 he published his "invention of antisepsis." The techniques required for ensuring a germ-free environment were elaborate, however, and most people couldn't be bothered to follow them. Others were openly skeptical of his theories, and it was thus many years before physicians widely practiced his suggestions. By 1890, Robert Koch (1843–1910) discovered that steam could be used to disinfect surgical instruments.

William Stewart Halsted (1852–1922) has been called the father of American surgery. He was one of the first Americans to see the value in sterilizing equipment, and he introduced the use of rubber gloves in surgery. Halsted has been remembered for many things, including his lifelong battle to break free from drug addiction. Despite his addiction (probably acquired from experimenting with the newly discovered wonder drug, cocaine), he helped plan The Johns Hopkins Medical School, a distinctly different educational model, combining the university concept with the hospital and its ready supply of learning experiences. Halsted became the first to teach surgery there; he also introduced the idea of residency training programs, which dramatically altered the course of medical education. Finally Halsted took the stopwatch out of the operating room. Surgeons had prided themselves on how fast they could amputate a limb or suture a wound, which might have been practical in the days before anesthesia. Halsted, however, told his students to slow down, that "tissues treated with kindness respond better than tissues treated with haste."

MIRACLES OF DIAGNOSIS

The nineteenth and twentieth centuries saw rapid advances in medicine. As doctors' knowledge increased, so did scientific discoveries. Modern medicine has been forever changed by these inventions and discoveries. Wilhelm Roentgen (1845–1923, a German physics professor) invented the x-ray in 1895. Until then doctors could not see inside a body to determine the extent of disease or damage. With the x-ray, this became possible. In 1898, chemists figured out the analgesic qualities of willow bark and meadowsweet, and marketed aspirin.

In 1924 Willem Einthoven (1860–1927) developed the electrocardiograph, or EKG, a machine that can detect heart damage, even pinpointing the parts affected. The year 1935 was notable for two reasons. First, with the introduction of a working model of a heart and lung machine, surgeons were enabled to work on a heart. Sulfa drugs were also discovered in 1935, which finally made possible the defeat of bacterial infections. Sulfa drugs slowed the growth of bacteria enough that the patient's body could marshal its defenses to overwhelm the infection. While Alexander Fleming (1881–1955) actually discovered penicillin in 1928, the year 1941 first saw its use in combatting sepsis. Far more potent than sulfa drugs, it could prevent death from abscesses and could cure gonorrhea. America guarded the secret of penicillin—needed to protect its troops during World War II—as jealously as it guarded work on the atomic bomb. Because the Germans and Japanese did not learn of penicillin until much later, one saw more amputees in those countries directly after the war.

In 1953 the first heart and lung machine was used in an operation. That year also saw the marketing of the polio vaccine devised by Jonas Salk (1914–1992). A year later, the marketing of Thorazine dramatically changed the lives of people suffering from schizophrenia. Until then such people were institutionalized because of their unpredictable, often combative behavior. While Thorazine was not a cure for schizophrenia (to date, there is none), it erased or minimized the delusions and hallucinations, allowing patients to live more normal lives outside the hospital confines. Thorazine made possible more humane treatment of the mentally ill; in some cases, it replaced restraints and lobotomies.

On December 3, 1967, Dr. Christiaan Barnard performed the first heart transplant in the world—in South Africa. That one operation and its success gave hope to people dying from heart disease and the possibility of adding months and even years to their lives. Almost fifteen years later to the day, Dr. William De Vries implanted an artificial heart in Barney Clark—the first permanent heart replacement. With the introduction of the drug Cyclosporine in the 1980s, the body became less likely to reject life-saving transplants. By the 1990s, transplants had become an almost everyday procedure.

Other new diagnostic tools are the CAT scanner (computerized tomography) from the 1970s, (which reduced the number of exploratory surgeries being done), and from the 1980s the NMR (nuclear magnetic resonance) and MRI (magnetic resonance imaging). The year 1978 saw the birth of the first test-tube baby, which ushered in a whole new era of babies conceived in artificial ways.

And, of course, on January 22, 1973, the U.S. Supreme Court decision in *Roe* v. *Wade* legalized abortion in the United States. Doctors here could finally perform abortions without risk of being stripped of their medical licenses or imprisoned. Hippocrates might have objected to the turn of events, since he specifically forbade a doctor to perform an abortion, but many doctors today believe that they must adapt to the times.

11

As some see it, it is not a question of *whether* there will be abortions, but *what kind* of abortions. Clearly, modern medicine presents more ethical dilemmas for doctors than at any other time in history.

With the discovery of the HIV virus and AIDS (for which there presently is no cure), being a doctor—taking care of patients who harbor this disease—took on a dangerous new quality.

2

Qualities of a Good Doctor

Anyone with the right connections, enough money, and the brains to get through medical school can become a doctor. It takes a lot more, however, to become a "good" doctor, which is what we shall examine in this chapter. Perhaps you already possess some of the qualities we shall consider; if so, you're one step ahead of the game. But even if you don't possess every sterling quality mentioned here, it doesn't mean you're banned from the profession. You can cultivate some of those qualities, particularly with the right experiences. Remember, too, that certain qualities apply to certain medical specialties. If, for example, you don't enjoy patient contact, you can still be a doctor practicing in one of the areas where the doctor doesn't deal with patients directly. If you don't have much manual dexterity, you choose a specialty other than surgery. Profit and prestige may be by-products of doctoring, but they should not be your motivating force. Good doctors are motivated more by compassion and desire to help others. The medical profession is a *service* profession; it was never intended as a quick way to earn a buck. If you have no interest in helping people, you'd be well advised to look into a different line of work. The patient who comes to you for help wants to believe that he or she matters to you. If he's going to entrust you with his life, or his child's, he wants to know that you have an investment, too. People can sense it when you're working only to earn a living.

Showing **compassion** for people means seeing beyond the physical symptoms they present. The good doctor truly cares about the families he treats, obeys the law by reporting abuse when he sees it, and recognizes the emotional burden of prolonged hospitalization. As an advocate for the patient, he has to understand that patient's needs. He can't do that well without compassion.

Naturally, you need to be **intelligent** to become a doctor. Not necessarily the valedictorian of your class, but certainly bright enough in high school to get into college and then into medical school. Surviving in medical school (where students are literally bombarded with information) requires above-average intelligence and **initiative**. You may be smart, but if you don't get your work done, you won't make the grade. Intelligence also involves a certain degree of **resourcefulness**. You need not know the answer to a problem, but you do need to know where to start looking.

A healthy level of **initiative** will get you through the admissions process of medical school. You have to stay on top of **what** information you've sent to **which** schools, and **which** schools have responded. Otherwise, you'll never keep track of the enormous amount of paperwork and forethought that are part of getting admitted. Once admitted, it takes initiative to keep up with your schoolwork. Those who learn the most are usually the ones who arrange to do so.

Along the same vein, it helps to be **independent**. As a doctor, more often than not you are your own boss. If you can't make decisions without constantly consulting your colleagues, you'll probably need a group practice that will indulge your insecurity.

Doctors need **patience** in every aspect of their jobs. You may find yourself two hours behind schedule; you may be researching that elusive cure for AIDS; you may be facing a triple bypass operation that isn't going according to plan. In no case can you hurry the results. Fuming will only stress you further. Working in haste often results in mistakes; mistakes in the medical realm can be fatal.

The doctor who is patient will survive the demands on his schedule and the assaults on her ego. If you worry that you don't have much patience, don't despair. Medical school will no doubt teach you "delayed gratification," which is a form of patience. Becoming a doctor takes time. If it doesn't kill you, delaying the rewards builds character.

One quality you can work on right now while you're in high school is your **listening skills**. Doctors learn most of what it takes to diagnose patients by listening to their complaints. The doctor who is too rushed to listen or thinks he doesn't need to listen will miss important information. Sometimes, **listening** is the best medicine there is. And in psychiatry, it's your *job*!

The reverse side of good listening skills is good **communication skills**. Daily you will be sharing information with colleagues, advising patients, reporting to insurance companies, and possibly testifying in court. If you can't get your message across, you won't reach anyone. Learning to communicate clearly is something you can work on right now. And while you're boning up on your communication skills, spend a moment more practicing your penmanship. There's no reason for doctors to write illegible prescriptions.

Doctors need a lot of **energy**, and not just to get through medical school and residency training. Of

15

course, that's where they'll need it first. Medical school is exhausting (as well as exhilarating and challenging). After graduation, it's even worse. Most interns learn to function on four hours of sleep on average; some nights they don't get any. With an eighty-hour workweek (at minimum), time needed for studying, and occasional weekends devoted to moonlighting, you can see why someone would need a little energy.

Once you're out in the "real world" of medicine, you can structure your practice around your energy level. Energetic doctors can take on emergency medicine and surgery; those who prefer less hectic schedules might consider radiology or part-time family practices. Don't think that psychiatry requires less energy because the people are sitting down all the time. Psychiatry is one of the most emotionally demanding of the professions.

Students used to competing have an easier time in medical school. Getting into medical school is fraught with **competition**; staying in sometimes means "besting" your fellow students. Even after medical school, you compete for the best training programs and the best practice opportunities. If you go into private practice later on, you'll still be competing for your client population. If you hate competing, but survive medical school anyway, you can always select a less competitive environment in which to practice.

While you don't have to have a **sense of humor** to practice medicine, it helps you keep things in perspective. If you can laugh at some of the flotsam life throws your way (like unappealing patients, demanding insurance companies, and hours of paperwork), your own health will be the better for it. If you take yourself too seriously, you'll be crestfallen the first time something doesn't go according to plan.

Two words of advice: A sense of humor is not the

same as sarcasm. And laughing **at** people is not the same as laughing **with** them.

All doctors are going to have to make **decisions** about patient care. Sometimes those decisions will be life and death matters. You have to be able to make decisions—sometimes snap decisions—and stand by them. They won't always be right. No doctor is immune from error, but he or she must be confident enough to take mistakes in stride. Making decisions about a patient's care may mean stopping treatment; it may mean overruling a family's wishes. The doctor, weighing all the facts, ultimately acts on his best judgment. If you don't have the strength to make these decisions day in and day out, this is not the job for you.

Patients will die under your care—even when you've done everything to help them. If and when that happens, it'll be your job to tell the families. As the doctor, you could delegate the task to somebody else, but the family members will want to hear this news from you. As long as you are not intimidated by anger and grief, you can face these unhappier tasks. Having a good handle on your own feelings keeps you from being overwhelmed by those of others.

At times you may have to confront people when you suspect abuse. As the patient's advocate, you have to be willing to question his caregivers and report your suspicions. That's obviously not the "fun" part of being a doctor, but it's crucial to the patient's well-being.

More than anything else, however, a doctor needs **integrity**. A patient shows his most vulnerable self to his doctor. He not only bares his body, but often his soul as well. He tells the doctor things he may never have told another person in his life. And he can tolerate this much

17

vulnerability only if he trusts the doctor not to abuse the relationship. A doctor, then, has to know how to keep confidences and—in the case of abuse or danger—when to break them. She or he knows the boundaries and will not seek to sexualize the doctor/patient relationship, no matter how tempting the opportunity. When faced with an ethical dilemma, the doctor acts on principles. A doctor without principles obviously has none to fall back on. . . .

Most doctors need a good measure of **equanimity** to deal with all the surprises of medical practice. By the end of residency training, nothing should shock you anymore. If you tend to overreact to emergencies, you'll end up panicking your patients.

Doctors need a keen eye. Tracking down the cause of disease often means looking beyond the obvious.

Surgeons assert that surgery is an art, that you have to be skilled with your hands to practice this specialty, Certainly, if you lack manual dexterity, you'd be a poor surgeon, and would be well advised to choose a different field of medicine.

The good doctor walks a fine line between conceit and humility. We all want our doctors to be self-confident, to know what they're doing, but we'd like to think they know their limitations. **Humility**, then, goes hand in hand with **confidence**. Doctors need to be able to consult others without seeing it as an admission of failure. But they must also believe in their abilities because they literally hold people's lives in their hands. **Conceit** gives them the courage to operate; humility keeps them from overstepping their bounds.

And if you haven't figured it out by now, getting to be a doctor requires **perseverance**. Only those who can hang in there will eventually make it to the top.

It's a good idea to volunteer in a hospital (or make it your summer job, if you need the money) well before embarking on medical training. That way you can find out if you like the environment. Most doctors will be glad to talk to you about their job if they know you are interested in it. Don't hesitate to ask them what they like (best and least) about their medical practices.

And don't forget your hobbies. Doctors need an outlet, too, and a life outside of medicine.

3

Educational Requirements

To get into medical school, you first have to spend three, or more typically four, years in college. Contrary to popular opinion, you do not have to major in one of the sciences to gain admission to medical school. Admissions people are equally interested in the well-rounded student who understands politics and people and can communicate well. That may be someone who majored in history and government, in sociology or psychology, or in English. Of course, you still must take the basic science courses in college: organic and inorganic chemistry (with labs), general biology or zoology (with labs), and general physics (with lab). Many doctors complain that these science courses were not helpful in preparing for a career in medicine, but they are required.

Getting into medical school takes some serious planning. First, you need to get into college. Students are advised to try to go to a college in the state where they want to attend medical school. (Often the medical schools give preference to in-state applicants.) Many students consider the undergraduate years relatively unimportant—what counts is simply the grade point average. That line of thinking has a large flaw. You do have to concentrate on your grade point average because it does influence your chances of getting into medical school. On the off chance that you don't get into medical school, however, you ought to have a bachelor's degree that can lead to some other career. Take the necessary science courses, but major either in something that interests you (after all, you ought to have fun in college) or that has other job possibilities. (And if you are accepted and end up hating the medical profession, you'll still have something to fall back upon.)

When choosing a college, consider the expense as well as the location and the degree opportunities. You'll be saddled with an enormous medical school debt; there's no need to burden yourself further by attending the most expensive undergraduate college.

While you're in college, work hard, but have some fun. No telling when you'll have this much free time again. Cultivate outside interests; join a fraternity or sorority (preferably one that's service-oriented), or play organized sports. Remember, you'll always need something outside of medicine to sustain you; otherwise, you'll be a slave to your work. (Besides, the extra-curricular activities look good on your application form.)

Cultivate your relationships with your professors. No, not for dating purposes. You're going to need at least a couple of recommendations to medical school. Naturally, you'll want them from those professors who know you best and will write favorably. Share with them your goals for medical school long before you need their recommendation. Perhaps they can advise you on courses and activities. They might introduce you to other influential instructors. Professors set aside office hours so that students can see them about schoolwork or problems. Take advantage of this opportunity. When professors know you better, they'll be better able to write that glowing recommendation.

21

CHOOSING A SCHOOL

Start narrowing down your choice of medical schools in your junior year of college. Visit the campuses; talk to students already enrolled. They may tell you things that the school's brochure leaves out. In the meantime, prepare to take the MCAT exam. Just as most colleges require SAT or ACT scores, most medical schools require the MCAT. This test takes about six hours and is divided into four parts: verbal reasoning (85 minutes), physical sciences (100 minutes), a writing sample (60 minutes), and biological sciences (100 minutes). Medical schools give a lot of weight to the scores, so you're best advised to prepare in earnest for the exam. Practice books on the MCAT abound; check out your local library or bookstore. You can buy *Barron's Guide to Medical and Dental Schools* for $13.95, and it includes a sample test to get you used to the format. Many communities offer preparatory courses; you'll have to decide how much of an effort you need to make. As in studying for any exam, you'll retain more information if you schedule short study sessions over a long period of time, rather than trying to cram in eight-hour marathons the week before the exam. Take the test in the spring of your junior year; if you do poorly, you can take it again your senior year.

THE INTERVIEW

Your next hurdle is the admissions interview. After you've sent your applications to your preferred medical schools, you wait around for an invitation to be interviewed. Sometimes, only 30 percent of applicants are interviewed, so that in itself is an honor. Remember, you're competing with hundreds of other equally qualified students. You can't afford to treat the interview lightly. As with the exam, *prepare*, so you can present yourself in the best possible light. Consider typical questions you might be asked and rehearse your responses. (But don't wind up *sounding* as if you've rehearsed.) Know why you want to be a doctor; be able to explain any perceived weaknesses you have (such as low MCAT scores, average grades in the sciences); and remember your strengths. It is not conceit to mention them. Strange as it may sound, *know your major field of study*. One pre-med student who happened to be a government major couldn't recall his state legislators on the day of his interview. Had he known that his interviewer would fault him for the lapse, he would have explained that his focus of study had been theory, not state government. But he didn't explain, and the interviewer drew his conclusions, and the young man didn't get into medical school.

On the day of your interview (and you'll probably have more than one interview, with more than one person each time), dress appropriately. This isn't the time to make either a fashion or a political statement. Dressing appropriately means dressing conservatively. For men, it probably means a sports jacket and tie; for women, it probably means a dress that reveals neither cleavage nor thigh. Don't be flip in the interview; be respectful even if you don't like the interviewers. If you're nervous, acknowledge it and go on. Chances are, they've noticed. Sometimes it takes the pressure off to be upfront about it.

COSTS

If your greatest worry about medical school is the cost, not the admissions process, let us assure you that you don't have to be wealthy to attend. Every medical school has a financial aid office, and the people there can explain the various loans and scholarships that are available to fund your education. Keep in mind that a

23

scholarship is a gift; it doesn't have to be repaid. A loan, on the other hand, does, and it accumulates interest.

Some loans, like the Guaranteed Student Loans and the Health Professions Student Loans, do not accumulate interest until you have completed medical training (which is when you'll have to start repaying the loan.) Other loans, like Supplemental Loans for Students and Health Education Assistance Loans, start accruing interest immediately. Some loans have to be repaid upon graduation from medical school (which is a hardship on your paltry resident's earnings); some can wait until completion of your residency training. Do not be surprised to find that your medical school debt can exceed $100,000. Doctors have been managing this way for years. One of the medical community's complaints is that saddling students with such huge debt forces them to consider money first and foremost when they finish training. The need to repay their loans quickly drives some to consider higher-paying specialties for which they may not really be suited.

Of course, there are other ways to get through medical school without ending up in debt. If you don't mind repaying the military with several years of active service, look into joining the Navy, Army, or Air Force. They will finance your schooling. Many HMOs (health maintenance organization) are offering to pay doctors' medical school debts as a bonus for their signing on to work.

4

Medical School and Beyond

Men have long dominated the medical profession, but medical schools, more sensitized to this inequality, have been increasing their female enrollment. According to 1990–91 figures, women accounted for 38 percent of the students enrolled in medical school. How increasing the numbers of women will alter the experience of medical school remains to be seen.

SCHOOL EXPERIENCES

The first two years of medical school are typically devoted to classroom learning. Anatomy comes first, and with it the opportunity to examine your first cadaver. Anatomy lectures reportedly cover so much material that you'd be overwhelmed if you missed a class or skipped the reading. Most students are not sure they'll make it through medical school until they've successfully gotten by anatomy. To better learn the lessons of anatomy, you practice on a human cadaver in the lab. Some say that sharing the cadaver with four other people makes the experience less traumatic, but most agree that their first encounter with it upset them. No doubt, medical students' black humor springs from the need to make light of this unsettling experience. (You often hear of a student substituting himself for his buddy's cadaver. When his buddy pulls the cover off, the student sits up . . .) Nonetheless, by the end of the semester, students express gratitude to the people who donated their bodies to science. By dissecting the bodies and studying the relationship of the parts, these students have gotten a better picture of the inner workings of the human body.

Doctors have described medical school both as a wonderful learning experience and as an ordeal. Some saw it as challenging; others found it overwhelming. If you're able to memorize large amounts of material and can function on only six hours of sleep a night, you'll probably enjoy the experience. Your major problem will be disciplining yourself to study at every opportunity.

Medical school is not the time to begin a serious romance. You just won't have time for the other person. Some couples manage to drag out relationships, promising each other that "it'll be different after medical school." (But, ironically, more marriages founder during the residency years than during medical school.)

During those first two years, you learn how to conduct exams by experimenting on your colleagues. Most students appreciate the chance to practice on their fellow students. Real patients think the medical student, like the doctor she aspires to be, should know what she's doing. Other medical students know she doesn't . . . yet, anyway. And they're the ones who'll help you improve your technique.

ROTATION

You spend your last two years of medical school in "clinical clerkships." You rotate through the various medical specialties to practice what you've learned—and to learn what books can never adequately tell you. Spending a month in pediatrics, a month in internal medicine, a month in anesthesiology, for example, gives you a better feel for these jobs, enabling you to narrow down your choice of specialty. Sometimes you'll be expected to perform routine tasks (commonly called scutwork) just like the interns on the wards; other times you'll find yourself in the observer role. Usually, medical students end up doing as much as they volunteer to do. The more available you make yourself, the more you learn. Doctors have described these years as "rigorous, stimulating, with an almost unbearable workload."

During your third year of medical school, you should decide what type of doctor you want to be and start considering residency training programs. You'll want to apply to these programs by the beginning of your fourth year. You submit your choices of residency programs (in an accredited hospital), and the programs submit their list of candidates in order of preference. A computer matches up candidates and training programs, and students learn of their assignments in March of their senior year. Upon graduation from medical school, you are a doctor and can sign M.D. after your name.

However, that's only the beginning . . .

RESIDENCY

Depending on your medical specialty, the residency training program can last from three to seven years, with more for subspecialties. Typically, doctors spend four years in training. The first year of training, called the internship, starts in July and ends the following June. It is without question the most torturous year of training. If you think of the training years as a ladder, the internship constitutes the bottom rung. Interns, therefore, justifiably consider themselves exploited. The regular doctors (called attendings) delegate responsibilities to the chief residents, who delegate to the junior and senior residents, who delegate to the interns, who have no one to delegate. So *they* do most of the scutwork, which is frustrating, time-consuming, and boring after a while. Fortunately, they get very good at drawing blood and sticking tubes into the body; so by the end of their first year they're probably more adept at these routine procedures than the attendings. As the year passes, their confidence builds, and they begin to feel more like real doctors.

If a doctor's marriage is destined to fail, it'll usually falter during the years of residency training. And small wonder. Depending on which specialty you practice, you can end up being on call every three or four nights. Being on call may mean never leaving the hospital grounds that night, staying awake to monitor any problem and handle every admission. Try nurturing a relationship when you're exhausted and the only thing on your mind is getting a decent night's sleep. Try spending an evening out with your spouse when all you can think about are lab results on your newest patient and your grand rounds presentation the following day. Try having any sort of family life when you're away every third night, and when you *are* home you expect your husband to get up in the middle of the night to tend the kids.

Internship is the first time you get to practice being a real doctor. The bad news is you're considered the low man on the totem pole; the good news is that it only lasts a year. The following July, you're a resident.

In your second year, you're considered a junior resident; in the third year, a senior resident. As you progress up the ladder, your responsibilities increase, but you can delegate routine procedures to those you supervise. The hours remain long, although New York has legally restricted residents to practicing only 80 hours a week. That 80 hours does not include time spent studying or moonlighting for extra money on the weekends. And since residents and interns earn only about $20,000 a year, most need to bring in extra money. Residents do the same work as regular doctors in hospitals. They are responsible for their patients' care, and while they are supervised by the attending doctor, they are the ones who do the work: make the diagnosis, recommend and implement a treatment plan. Resident surgeons perform operations, and resident psychiatrists provide therapy. In private hospitals where patients have their own physicians, residents handle on-call duties and inform the attendings of any problems. Otherwise, residents are assigned routine admissions and are responsible for all the work that goes into healing that particular patient, conducting daily rounds and writing appropriate orders.

Internists and family practitioners finish their training after three years if they do not further specialize. (If they choose to practice a subspecialty, they will probably spend an additional two years in training, called a fellowship.) Surgeons enter longer training programs, typically two to four more years. Psychiatrists can spend their first year in internal medicine and the following three years in psychiatry. When you complete your training period, you're eligible to take the state medical exam for your license. When you've passed that exam, you're finally ready to set up practice.

CHOOSING A PRACTICE
Opportunities abound in the medical profession. You're limited only by your assets, your desire for certain hours, and your choice of location. Internists and family practitioners often choose to join a group practice (before launching a private practice), to save on the overhead and to benefit from the ready referral source. Psychiatrists often choose to open private practices in

the community where they have done their training (because of the contacts they've made). Radiologists and pathologists often choose to practice in the hospital, where they don't need to supply their own equipment or find referrals.

HMOs and other medical groups offer salaried positions to doctors, and often a bonus (a new car, repayment of medical school debt, use of a condo) for signing on for several years. For doctors who want more regular hours, HMOs offer job security and a chance to have a life outside the hospital. Others consider government employment or military employment for much the same reasons.

When considering which you want: a salaried position, group practice, or private practice, think about the type of commitment you're willing to make to your job. Do you want to be on call 24 hours a day because you have no one with whom to share the duty? Do you want the opportunity to see more patients and make more money? Do you want to be your own boss? Do you want to put in 80-hour workweeks?

WOMEN IN PRACTICE

How have women changed the practice of medicine? Women are typically drawn to internal medicine, pediatrics, family practice, psychiatry, and obstetrics. According to statistics in *American Medical News* (November 9, 1992), women earn 59 to 63 percent of the average male salary. Why? For one thing, women choose to practice in the lower-paying specialties. Second, they often see fewer patients than their male colleagues and work fewer hours. Some accept salaried positions, which are typically lower-paying. And finally, women have been allowed in numbers into the medical profession only in recent years. Thus, the statistics reflect the salary differentials of young women versus their older, more experienced male counterparts. As women gain more experience, compensation may reflect more equality.

If you're a woman reading this book, realize that you'll face certain special problems in the profession. As a woman, you'll be more likely confused with the nurses. Families will be more apt to call you "honey" and "dear" than they will your male colleague. You may face more power struggles with the staff, who sometimes are quicker to accept orders from a male doctor. And even though they're advised to view you all the same, many hospital administrators still consider women less reliable because of childrearing responsibilities. Women breaking into professions previously barred to them say they often feel compelled to work harder than the men, just to prove that they're equal to them. The result may be that they set inordinately high standards for other women to meet.

Many people applaud the number of women becoming doctors. Women, in general, seem to bring more empathy to their role and reportedly are more attentive to detail. They are also more interested in keeping regular hours.

Unfortunately, women still complain of sexual harassment, particularly as they try to break into the male-dominated specialties. Women need to sensitize others to this problem; men need to view women as colleagues, not conquests. In the end, one's gender should not be an obstacle to doing the work she's qualified to do.

5

Professional Organizations and Licensure

The American Medical Association (which boasts upwards of 300,000 members) was founded in 1846 to elevate the status of doctors by setting high standards for practice. It is also a powerful lobbying group. You can write the AMA for more information regarding the medical profession at 515 North State Street, Chicago, IL 60610.

You might also want to join your specialty's academy; they are listed in the second part of this book. Benefits of membership include prestige (getting to display your membership certificate), camaraderie, opportunities to attend educational workshops, and the monthly journals (outlining important research findings) and newsletters (noting regional meetings). These academies are not mandatory to join, nor are the various state organizations, but they're out there. Memberships are expensive (but tax-deductible), and you can join some as a medical student at reduced cost. When you find a specialty that particularly interests you, write to the academy for more information about the specialty and the training opportunities available.

BOARD CERTIFICATION

Choosing to become board-certified is a different matter. Although you are not required to be board-certified to practice medicine, many hospitals won't hire you unless you are. To obtain some forms of malpractice insurance, you have to be board-certified; if you plan to subspecialize, you must be board-certified, as well. Being board-certified is not the same as being licensed. When you've graduated from medical school and completed at least a year of residency training, you are eligible for licensure. Every state requires you to pass its written exam to be eligible to practice; the State Board of Medical Examiners offers the exam and grants the license. Many states offer the Federation Licensure Examination; if you have secured your license in that state by passing that exam, you are automatically granted your license in another state that uses the same exam. At the moment, there is no federal medical licensing law. If you do not adhere to certain principles, the State Board of Medical Examiners can revoke your license.

The difference again is that whereas licensing enables you to practice medicine, board certification further establishes your credentials. Acquiring certification is a rigorous process; though you are licensed by the state, you are certified by your profession. Upon graduation from an accredited medical school and the completion of residency training, you are eligible to take the written examination, which is administered several times a year in various locations. If you pass the written exam, in some cases you may then take the oral exam, and if you pass that part, you are granted certification. Some specialties require periodic recertification and/or participation in continuing education workshops. At the end of each chapter on the specialties, we've given the addresses of the boards of certification and the renewal requirements. If you practice a subspecialty, you'll need board certification in both the specialty (for example: internal medicine) and the subspecialty (geriatrics).

Joining several professional organizations and becoming board-certified is not the end of the road, however. Many doctors assume leadership roles in their communities. Naturally, it helps your practice to get involved in local projects and organizations; not only does it create goodwill, but it builds your referral base. More than that, though, it's important to get involved with others, to give something back to the community that supports you.

PART TWO

AN OVERVIEW OF JOBS IN MEDICINE

6

The Family Physician

SALARY
$100,000–$200,000 (depending on locale and type of practice).

YEARS OF RESIDENCY
3 years, which may or may not include a surgical rotation.

DESCRIPTION OF JOB
Years ago, doctors completed one year of internship following graduation from medical school and then went into general practice. Your parents or grandparents probably grew up with a G.P. who made housecalls when your folks were too sick to come to his office. The general practitioner handled an assortment of ills (childhood infections, minor injuries, diseases, heart attacks, and well-baby checks). Only when doctors began to specialize did the G.P. fall out of favor. Patients began to acquire their own internist, obstetrician and gynecologist, cardiologist, dermatologist, and urologist. They started viewing their bodies in isolated fashion. Not only were they sometimes uncertain which doctor should assess their complaint, but they began to feel less and

less connected to their doctors, none of whom they saw on a routine basis.

The major complaint with the general practitioner was that he had completed only one year of training, whereas other specialists had completed at least three. Most people didn't believe any doctor could know very much about any one thing if he only spent one year in generalized learning. Nonetheless, the need for a doctor to treat the whole person remained. Patients wanted one doctor to assess everything and to recommend specialists only as the need arose. And so the family physician evolved and in 1969 was officially recognized as a legitimate specialist in medicine.

The doctor who specializes in family practice is similar to the general practitioner but with more extensive training. As in similar specialties, he must train for three years after medical school. Unlike other specialists, he trains in all the areas, including a rotation through surgery. The family physician is then able to treat not only the whole person, but his whole family as well. A woman could see her family physician for a sore throat, a sprained ankle, and prenatal care. Even if she required a caesarean operation for delivery of that baby, she could still use her family physician. Once the baby was born, she'd continue seeing the same physician for its care.

The family physician treats a variety of problems, though he or she refers for more indepth treatment, if necessary. He or she offers emotional counseling, prescribes medication for infections, orders x-rays and blood tests, immunizes babies, and provides health care to nursing home residents. In short, he sees people from birth through old age, and treats the whole spectrum of diseases.

A typical day for a family physician might start out with rounds at 8:00 on hospitalized patients, checking on their progress, writing new orders, and notes in their charts. By 9:30 or so (perhaps when you think you're the first person he's seen that day), he'll start seeing private patients in his office. Because patients often want to talk about more than their presenting complaint, he starts falling behind schedule. Emergencies crop up through the day, and he squeezes them into the schedule. By late afternoon, after he's seen his last patient, he gets a message to call at the local nursing home because the blood pressure of one of his patients is too high. After tending to her, he goes home with his pager for dinner. Several times during the evening, he's paged. Once a pregnant patient has a bad headache and wants to know what medicine she can safely take. A father wants to know what chicken pox looks like. A two-month-old infant is running a 102-degree fever. The doctor decides to see that patient at the hospital—it's now 9:00.

A family physician can have a private practice, a group practice, or a salaried position with an HMO. Whether employed in a solo practice or a group, he or she can still share on-call duties with another doctor, which provides an evening off every so often. The doctors can be employed by the government and the military. As primary care physicians, they are in the highest demand and will continue to be in the near future.

QUALITIES NEEDED
In this type of medical practice, you need the ability to get along well with people, or what's called a "good bedside manner." You will not endear yourself to others (and thus increase your practice) if you're gruff with patients. You can't demonstrate compassion if you don't feel any, so if you just don't "click" with people, you're better advised to choose a different specialty.

You need a keen eye and the patience it sometimes takes to uncover the real problem. You need good listening skills, because diagnosis so often rests on what the patient tells you—and sometimes because what your patients need most is a good ear and the time to share their grief. Along with good listening skills, you need good communication skills because you'll be advising your patients on how to get better, as well as consulting with colleagues. Patients are notorious for not complying with treatment expectations; part of the problem is they don't always understand what the doctor wants them to do. If you can't get your message across to your patients, they won't understand, and if they don't understand, they won't comply with the treatment strategy. It's as simple as that.

Family physicians must also be decisive and confrontive. Being on call requires you to make some snap decisions over the telephone. Dealing with families means you'll no doubt encounter signs of abuse with some people. If you uncover abuse, you have the obligation to confront the caregivers and then report your suspicions. You may be additionally required to testify in court.

Finally, you need great energy for this job (unless you can work out a part-time arrangement, or accept a salaried position).

ADVANTAGES

It's rewarding to earn the respect of your community. It's nice to be paid so well for doing work you find both enjoyable and challenging. Curing infections, reducing suffering, and delivering babies bring a sense of accomplishment and, of course, gratitude. It's nice to be appreciated. Other good points: the malpractice insurance rates are low in this specialty, and it's easy to find a job. Opportunities for this primary-care physician are everywhere. Even in HMOs, the need is greatest for doctors who will examine the patient first and make suitable referrals only when necessary. Finally, you'll develop long relationships with people, seeing whole families over the course of a lifetime. You won't be forced to stop seeing a client simply because he has grown too old.

DISADVANTAGES

In all professions there's a downside. You simply have to weigh the advantages and disadvantages. With this specialty, and especially if you're in private practice, you may find yourself working more than you'd like. Too much time is spent away from your family. There's too much paperwork (although this is true in every medical specialty) and too much bureaucratic intervention. Independent insurance groups have determined the reimbursement value of various procedures and office visits, and you are at their whim. Unfortunately, "procedures" (such as x-rays and tests) are reimbursed at a higher rate than mere office visits, and so you're compensated less because you do more office visits than procedures.

You may have to make some ethical decisions, such as whether or not to resuscitate that 95-year-old Alzheimer's patient after her second heart attack, or how to tell a severely depressed patient that he has an incurable form of cancer. Likewise, you'll have to decide how much free medical advice and prescriptions you're willing to dole out to your relatives and friends.

As in all medical practice these days, you face the constant threat of an expensive, damaging malpractice suit. The possibility always exists that a patient will sue you for an unsatisfactory outcome of treatment. Even if you win your case or opt to settle out of court, your reputation will be tarnished. People will remember the allegations long after they've forgotten the outcome of the case. The only thing you can do is carry adequate insurance and practice good medicine. Some surveys show that doctors who spend the most time with their patients, explaining treatment and outcomes, are the least likely to get sued.

PROFESSIONAL ORGANIZATION
The American Academy of Family Physicians
8880 Ward Parkway
Kansas City, MO 64114-2797

BOARD OF CERTIFICATION
American Board of Family Practice, Inc.
2228 Young Drive
Lexington, KY 40505-4294

(Requires recertification after six years.)

7

The Internist

SALARY
$95,000–$200,000 (the upper end reflects specialization)

YEARS OF RESIDENCY
3 years in internal medicine

2 to 3 additional years in a specialized area (for example, geriatrics, sports medicine, oncology, hematology, rheumatology, nephrology, and cardiology)

DESCRIPTION OF JOB
The internist (not to be confused with the intern) may sound like a family physician, but her focus is more specialized. As a rule, she does not see children or provide prenatal care. Remember, she has spent three years studying internal medicine, unlike the family physician who has spent three years studying various areas of medicine. The internist may perform minor surgery (removing warts, lancing boils) but she usually does not have the training to do more significant procedures.

Many internists specialize, spending an extra two to three years in training. Obviously, they know a great deal more about their specialty than the family physician, and for that reason alone, many people choose an internist as their primary care physician.

Internists do many of the same things family physicians do. They diagnose and treat illness (from headaches, to sore throats, to swollen, aching joints) and disease (including cancer, heart disease, and AIDS). Some of their tasks vary according to the specialty practiced. For example, oncologists diagnose and treat cancer patients; they manage the chemotherapy and coordinate the treatments with radiologists, who provide the radiation therapy. Geriatric specialists spend a lot of time in nursing homes, managing a myriad of physical problems and regulating anywhere from six to sixteen medications. Nephrologists see patients complaining of kidney ailments and coordinate treatment with radiologists and possibly surgeons.

Internists consult with other doctors, especially with radiologists, who can explain the x-ray results and CAT scans; they make referrals for surgery and consult pathologists about the results of tissue samples. Internists routinely make disability determinations (when patients seek a doctor's confirmation that they are unable to work) and provide care to patients in nursing homes. They also monitor abuse, carefully questioning the caregivers about their suspicions and reporting abuse to the appropriate authorities.

A typical day for an internist may sound similar to the family physician's day. She probably starts at an equally early hour, checking on hospitalized patients, assessing their progress, and determining their readiness for discharge. She writes any new orders in the chart, and notes the patient's progress. By 9:30 or so, she's ready to see her first office patient, who may be an alchoholic man with liver problems. She not only has to diagnose the extent of his liver damage but address his continuing alchohol abuse. The next patient may be a college student who wants a prescription for birth control pills and needs a pelvic exam, too. While the doctor is examining her, the young woman mentions that she might have been exposed to AIDS. Not only might the internist then order a blood test to determine HIV status, but probably spend a few minutes talking to her about AIDS and safe sex.

Another patient may come in complaining of chest pain and end up talking about his marriage falling apart. The doctor not only examines him and orders the appropriate x-rays and EKGs, but additionally suggests counseling. In the meantime, the internist's nurse tells her that an elderly client with a history of phlebitis is on the phone, complaining of leg pain and difficulty walking. The doctor tells the patient to come in that day, and asks the nurse to fit her in the schedule. By now, she is behind schedule and barely has time to dictate her notes between patients. At the end of the day, she can look forward to an evening on call. If she goes out for dinner, her pager goes with her. (If she shares on-call duties with other doctors she probably will be on call only every third night or so. But she'll no doubt still carry her pager because it's an easy way for the hospital to reach her.)

QUALITIES NEEDED

An internist needs an inquisitive mind and a keen eye. To make a diagnosis, she needs to know a great deal about the specific symptoms; sometimes, she has to know how to draw this information out of patients. She's resourceful because some diseases don't respond to typical treatment strategies. And some patients don't respond to directives and admonishments.

Like any other doctor involved in patient contact, the internist needs good communication skills and good listening skills. She needs compassion to understand the patient's experience and to protect his confidentiality. She needs to be tough (confrontational), but warm (because her practice also depends a great deal on a "good bedside manner.") Some doctors think that if you're good at what you do, you can get away with discourtesy. It's not true. Patients often consider their internist to be their primary-care physician; if she is unfriendly, they'll trade her in.

Internists need to be a little obsessive because of all the paperwork involved. Then, too, they need to be self-starters because they won't have people standing over them telling them what to do each day.

ADVANTAGES

Internists also have lower than average malpractice insurance premiums. Finding cures for disease and lessening people's suffering is challenging, rewarding work. Challenging, if you like solving puzzles, and rewarding, because you're well compensated (relatively speaking) and accorded a high status in your community.

It's nice to be appreciated; it's nice to be considered an authority. There are also plenty of job opportunities for internists. You need never worry about being unemployed, and the choices are yours. You can embark on a solo practice or join a group (to keep down the overhead and share on-call duties). You can take a salaried position if you want more control over your hours.

DISADVANTAGES

Since internists spend a good amount of their practice talking to patients, they end up reimbursed at a lower rate than some other doctors. Independent insurance groups have determined the "cost" of certain procedures and office visits. For some reason, they've decided to reimburse the technological interventions more than the talking interventions. An internist might spend thirty minutes talking to a patient about his prognosis and be paid less than a doctor who runs a series of x-rays in a far shorter time.

Like all medical professions, the paperwork and bureaucratic interference take their toll. Internists have less time than some doctors to spend with families. It's hard to be married to someone whose job is so important and time-consuming.

Being an oncologist presents other problems. Because you're working with patients who have cancer, you will be dealing with death on an ongoing basis. If you believe that suffering—not death—is the enemy here, you may be better able to handle the stress. Often death is welcomed over continued pain. Nonetheless, you'll have chosen a field in which your patients commonly die despite your interventions.

As a geriatric specialist, you'll encounter Alzheimer's and other forms of dementia (that are presently incurable). (If you can conceive of this specialty as challenging trying to maximize an elder's independence and function while decreasing the potential side effects of medication), the specialty can be rewarding.

Another disadvantage—for most of the medical specialties—is having to decide how to handle those relatives and friends who corner you at parties to ask for free medical advice and—worse—prescriptions.

Like the family physician, you'll face ethical dilemmas: when to resuscitate the elderly, dying patient, or when to recommend cessation of treatment on a comatose patient. If you know that two of your patients were intimate, and one is now HIV positive but wants to keep the information to himself, should you suggest that the other patient get a blood test?

Finally, like other doctors, you have to worry about a disgruntled patient suing you. The bad thing about the malpractice suit—even with a positive outcome—is that the public always remembers the allegations and not necessarily the outcome. Your reputation remains clouded. About the only thing you can do is make sure you're properly insured and that you practice good medicine. Spending time with your patients and making them fully aware of the possible outcomes of treatment strengthens the doctor/patient relationship and may prevent frivolous suits.

PROFESSIONAL ORGANIZATION
American Society of Internal Medicine
2011 Pennsylvania Avenue Suite 800
Washington, DC 20006-1808

BOARD OF CERTIFICATION
American Board of Internal Medicine
3624 Market Street
Philadelphia, PA 19104-2675
(Certificates are good for ten years.)

8

The Surgeon

SALARY
$200,000 and up (These are typically the highest-paid physicians; rates vary according to specialization practiced. Cardiovascular surgeons and neurosurgeons appear to have the highest incomes.)

YEARS OF RESIDENCY
5 years of surgical residency

2 to 3 additional years of training in a surgical sub-specialty

DESCRIPTION OF JOB
This category of medicine is not easily described because it encompasses so many specializations. There are cardiovascular surgeons (who work on the heart and blood vessels), neurosurgeons (who work on the brain and spinal cord), orthopedic surgeons (who work on the musculoskeletal system), thoracic surgeons (who work on the chest), urologists (who work on the urethra, bladder and kidneys), ophthalmologists (who work on the eyes), otolaryngologists (who work on the ears, nose, and throat) and plastic surgeons (who perform recon-

structive and cosmetic surgery). What they all have in common is the ability to do surgery.

All surgeons coordinate their treatments with reports of radiologists and anesthesiologists. Let's look at each of these specialists separately.

The **cardiovascular surgeon** treats damaged valves and abnormalities within the heart. She performs bypass operations on blocked coronary arteries, repairs aneurysms, and possibly transplants hearts.

The **neurosurgeon** treats brain tumors (not all of which are malignant), tumors of the pituitary gland and of the spinal cord. He repairs aneurysms, treats spina bifida and hydrocephalus, and operates to control seizures. He also operates on head and spinal injuries brought about through accident or gunshot.

The **orthopedic surgeon** deals with the whole musculoskeletal system—bones, joints, muscles, cartilage, tendons, nerves, and ligaments. She treats clubfoot, scoliosis, bursitis, tendinitis, ruptured (or slipped) disks, dislocated kneecaps, hip dislocations, tumors or bone growths, and fractures suffered in accidents. She's the surgeon who would treat the youth who broke his leg skiing.

The **thoracic surgeon** deals with the chest cavity; sometimes, his roles have been taken over by the **cardiovascular surgeon** and the **pulmonary surgeon** (who specifically treats the lungs). The **urologist** treats everything having to do with the urinary tract and male sexual organs. He treats bladder infections (in both men and women), treats bladder and kidney stones, impotence, male sterility, and cancer of the urinary tract and the prostate. He also performs vasectomies.

The **ophthalmologist** treats abnormalities and diseases of the eye, including glaucoma, benign tumors, retinal tears and detachment, eye infections (like conjunctivitis, herpes simplex, and herpes zoster), cataracts (clouding of the lens of the eye), strabismus (crossed eyes), and eye injuries. Prescribing corrective lenses is the easiest part of his job.

The **otolaryngologist** treats ear infections, blockage of the Eustachian tube, inner-ear disease, Ménière's disease, otosclerosis, allergic rhinitis (inflammation of the nasal membranes), nasal obstructions, sinusitis, nosebleeds, tonsillitis, pharyngitis, and laryngitis. Microsurgery has allowed these doctors to repair damaged vocal cords, as well.

Plastic surgeons undergo the longest period of training before certification. Well known for their "nose jobs" (technically called nose contouring) and their breast augmentations and reductions, they are equally skilled at reconstructing the body following severe injury, reattaching limbs and parts of limbs, and improving the body's appearance.

The surgeon's life cannot be scheduled as easily as other doctors'. He or she performs many elective surgeries, but he has to be available for emergencies, as well. Many heart attacks occur in the early morning; car accidents happen at any hour of day and night.

The surgeon confers with other doctors regarding the feasibility of operating. She should be as skilled in knowing when to operate as knowing when it's not needed.

QUALITIES NEEDED
This specialty, more than most, requires both energy and stamina. Some surgeries last eight to twelve hours, and the most intricate can last even longer, the surgeon has to be able to "go the distance"; you can't quit in the middle just because you're tired. Surgeons need exquisite manual dexterity because much operating is an

art. You need to be resourceful, especially when the operation fails to go according to plan, and you need a lot of self-confidence. You hold people's lives in your hands. The neurosurgeon who is operating near the spinal column cannot afford to let his hand slip: one mismove will result in paralysis. The surgeon doing open-heart surgery can't afford to be indecisive, worried about how to tie off an aneurysm. The eye surgeon can't afford to be clumsy with his laser. So is arrogance just a by-product of the specialty? Neurosurgeon J. Kenyon Rainer summed it up this way, "Confidence keeps your hands steady; conceit keeps you confident." This is one job, then, where arrogance is not a deficit.

All doctors ought to have a good bedside manner, but it's less of a demand of the surgeon. Most people want an accomplished surgeon, and since they don't have to maintain a relationship with him or her, they can tolerate some brusqueness. For many surgeons, it helps to stay emotionally detached from the patient, particularly children. Surgeries are the highest-risk specialties; not all patients can survive your efforts to save them. If you're not emotionally involved with your patient, you'll be better able to take risks, to accept death if it should happen, and still want to practice surgery. Some surgeons need to be more personable, like the ophthalmologist, who regularly sees his patients for followup. The urologist needs to be sensitive to his patients' feelings; dealing with sexual issues requires skillful handling. These doctors, too, need both good listening and communication skills so that they note all pertinent information and explain surgical procedures in a way patients can understand.

Finally, surgeons need to know their limitations. Some things cannot yet be fixed; the good surgeon knows when *not* to operate, and when to refer to someone with greater skill.

ADVANTAGES

The surgical specialties are typically the highest paying. It's not uncommon for a surgeon to make upwards of $250,000 a year. Making that kind of money, surgeons naturally occupy positions of power and influence in the community, especially the medical community. They consider themselves "the doers" in the medical world because their job is to fix things, and it's easy to see when you've accomplished something in that respect. Broken legs are set, tumors are removed, and noses are contoured. Maybe you don't succeed in excising all the tumor, but you've given it your best shot. You did *something*. And when you've saved a person's life—especially a child's—the sense of accomplishment makes it all worthwhile.

To say the least, the work is challenging and exciting. Job opportunities abound for the surgeon. You'll always have a steady supply of patients as long as there are injuries to repair, tumors to remove, and organs to be transplanted.

Finally, like some of the other specialties (for example, ophthalmology), you'll have more regular hours.

DISADVANTAGES

Surgery is risky work. Sometimes your patient dies, and you may feel responsible. The pressure to save lives and the intricacies of some operations make this a high-stress specialty, with burnout a common result. Because it is risky work, your malpractice premiums will be exceedingly high (depending on your specialty, of course; ophthalmology is not as high as neurosurgery). These high rates reflect the surgeon's greater likelihood of being sued. Doctors make mistakes, but people no longer want to accept them. Surgeons are not supposed to "fail." As we've noted in other sections, no doctor can afford a malpractice suit. Even if the jury finds in

53

his favor, the public will remember the allegations a lot longer than they will the result. Continuing malpractice suits will tarnish the surgeon's reputation. Fear of a negative outcome may make some surgeons too cautious in the future, less willing to take on a high-risk patient.

Surgeons have demanding and unpredictable work schedules, which means they don't get much time home with their families. Emergencies occur at all hours, and if you're on call and paged to surgery, it won't matter that you're in the middle of your daughter's sixth birthday party. One problem with gaining a good reputation is ending up in high demand. Your hours at home seem to dwindle to nothing. . . .

Surgeons risk exposure to AIDS, since blood is involved in surgery. Despite gloved hands and covered bodies, surgeons can still encounter contaminated fluids.

Surgeons face ethical dilemmas: Will operating only prolong suffering? Which of two deserving candidates gets the liver transplant?

And finally, bear in mind that this is one specialty in which so far the men greatly outnumber the women.

PROFESSIONAL ORGANIZATIONS

American Academy of Ophthalmology
P.O. Box 7424
San Francisco, CA 94120-7424

The American Academy of Otolaryngology,
   Head and Neck Surgery
One Prince Street
Alexandria, VA 22314

BOARDS OF CERTIFICATION
The American Board of Plastic Surgery, Inc.
Seven Penn Center
Suite 400
1635 Market St.
Philadelphia, PA 19103-2204

The American Board of Surgery, Inc.
1617 John F. Kennedy Boulevard
Philadelphia, PA 19103-1847
(Recertification is voluntary.)

The American Board of Ophthalmology
111 Presidential Boulevard
Bala Cynwyd, PA 19004
(Must complete a designated renewal program every ten
years to maintain certification.)

The American Board of Otolaryngology
5615 Kirby Drive
Houston, TX 77005

9

The Psychiatrist and Neurologist

SALARY
$100,000–$170,000 (Neurologists usually command higher salaries, but the figure varies greatly, depending on whether one is in private practice or in a salaried position, and to some extent on the locale in which you practice. Administrative work is also better reimbursed.)

YEARS OF RESIDENCY
1 year internship in internal medicine or pediatrics, plus

3 years of psychiatry

or

4 years of psychiatry or neurology training

One can also be certified in both specialties at once.

DESCRIPTION OF JOB
If you saw the movies "Ordinary People" or "Prince of Tides" you have some idea what a psychiatrist does. If

he's in private practice, he sees patients in his office for a variety of problems. Not all psychiatrists have their patients stretch out on a couch to relate their problems. Some just sit facing each other, and anyone looking in on the scene might think they were having a pleasant conversation, albeit a one-sided one. You see, the psychiatrist is trained to listen more than he talks, so the patient appears to do all the talking. Psychiatrists also prescribe medication because many psychological disorders result from biochemical disturbances. People who are depressed often have low levels of a chemical called serotonin in the brain, as do people with obsessive compulsive disorder (a disorder that causes people to think repetitious thoughts and engage in rituals, like handwashing). Medications such as Prozac help restore their serotonin levels. With the incurable disorder schizophrenia, the brain appears to produce too much dopamine; medications control the delusions and hallucinations that patients experience by reducing the dopamine levels.

Psychiatrists also practice in hospitals, either in a private psychiatric hospital or in a psychiatric ward of a regular hospital. In that setting, they are responsible for diagnosing each patient and instituting a treatment plan. Usually, the psychiatrist makes "rounds" of his patients with the nurse and social worker. These other professionals can advise him of any family problems and how the patient is responding to treatment. The psychiatrist monitors the patient's blood level (to maintain the drug in a therapeutic range if his patient is on antidepressant medication or lithium) and orders CAT scans and EEGs as needed to determine any neurological problems. If a severely depressed patient needs shock treatment (called ECT), he orders that as well. (Incidentally, shock treatment is not the horrific experience you saw in the movie "One Flew Over The Cuckoo's Nest." Nowadays, the patient is adequately sedated so that he does not ex-

57

perience discomfort. ECT works because it increases levels of Gaba, serotonin, and norepinephrine in the brain. Low levels of serotonin and norepinephrine have been associated with depression.) The psychiatrist provides counseling, and records patients' progress in their charts. He may consult other doctors (typically neurologists for CAT scan results, psychologists for testing data) and work up a case to present at grand rounds. His day is not over at 5:00 either. The psychiatrist, too, is on call, since people don't confine their emotional crises to regular working hours. If a person comes to the hospital seeking admission (because he's hearing voices or feeling suicidal), the psychiatrist needs to evaluate him.

The forensic psychiatrist evaluates criminals (to determine mental status and sanity) for the courts, and he is naturally called upon to testify.

In the hospitals, you're probably more apt to see the most severely disturbed patients, but even in private practice, you'll have your share of suicidal patients and sociopaths.

The neurologist is best thought of as a consultant. She helps to diagnose the patient thought to have neurological versus psychological problems. She may treat or diagnose migraine headaches, temporal arteritis, arteriosclerosis, aneurysms, epilepsy, brain tumors, Parkinson's disease, dementia, and multiple sclerosis. She would want to refer her patients with tumors and aneurysms to a neurosurgeon, who could then operate. She would act as the primary physician for patients diagnosed with Parkinson's and multiple sclerosis, managing their neurological symptoms with the appropriate medication. The neurologist's hours are probably more regular than the psychiatrist's, and definitely more regular than the neurosurgeon's.

Qualities Needed

The psychiatrist needs good listening skills and communication skills because so much of her work derives from close patient contact. To learn what she needs to know about a patient, she has to listen more than she talks. Her job is to help the patient sort out his problems, not to fill him full of her advice.

The psychiatrist needs to convey warmth, understanding, and trustworthiness. Because patients will bare their souls to her, she must be able to keep confidences and maintain appropriate boundaries. That means not acting on an impulse to sexualize the relationship.

Since she deals with people's feelings, she needs to be comfortable examining and sharing her own. You can't help someone through the grief process if you're afraid to look at your own. Helping someone express his anger means being able to express your own appropriately. You must keep your own problems separate from the patient's.

The psychiatrist needs courage (to confront patients about self-destructive behavior) and stamina (because therapy is often a long, emotionally draining process). She needs patience (because therapy is a slow process as well) and resourcefulness (because patients often resist the very help they seek). Like the other specialists she needs an obsessive tendency to stay on top of her paperwork.

The neurologist also needs both good listening and good communication skills; consulting with colleagues about difficult cases demands it. He needs a good bedside manner, but because his patient contact is more limited than the psychiatrist's, it is not as crucial to his success. He does need an eye for detail in order to make the proper diagnosis.

ADVANTAGES

Both psychiatry and neurology are challenging, well-paid specialties. The liability insurance rates for both are low, and the hours are more regular than for many doctors. Compared to the other specialties, malpractice suits are less likely.

Because no special equipment is needed to practice psychiatry, the overhead is low. (Neurology is a different story unless you refer your patients to the hospital for diagnostic procedures.)

Psychiatry may not seem like a medical job because you don't have to wear a white lab coat or carry around a stethoscope, but for some people, that's its advantage. It doesn't have to be practiced in a hospital setting either.

Except for places like New York City and Washington D.C. (where the market is saturated), you have plenty of opportunity to set up a practice. Salaried positions in hospitals abound, too, if you want more predictable hours.

DISADVANTAGES

It's harder in these two specialties than the others to sense accomplishment. If someone breaks a leg, the surgeon puts a cast on it. If someone gets pneumonia, the doctor treats it with antibiotics and the lungs clear. If someone is depressed, on the other hand, no one readily sees what's wrong because the disturbance isn't always visible on the outside. Talking out the problems is a slow process, and there isn't always a moment in time when the psychiatrist thinks, "Aha, this patient is now cured." Neurologists can lessen the symptoms of their patients with Parkinson's disease or multiple sclerosis, but a cure does not yet exist for either.

Emotionally disturbed patients can be demanding, unreasonable, and sometimes dangerous. So can their families, who often expect instant cures. It's not easy treating a psychotic patient who might kill himself or someone else because he was not adequately medicated or institutionalized. The stress of dealing with such individuals (and their family members) can lead to burnout.

The paperwork can turn you off, too. You have to document treatment plans, medical orders, and progress notes. You have to fill out insurance forms and requests for x-rays and EEGs, not to mention writing admission histories and discharge summaries.

Psychiatrists and neurologists are sometimes looked down upon by other members of the medical profession because they don't necessarily "do" anything. Neurologists **refer**. . . . Psychiatrists **listen**. . . .

Nonetheless, relatives and acquaintances will still call you up for advice and prescriptions, from antibiotics to benzodiazepines. You'll have to decide how many problems you want to listen to and how many prescriptions you want to write. . . . There will be other ethical dilemmas, too—like what to do with information you hear from one patient that impacts on another patient.

Because this work is high stress, and psychiatrists prescribe a lot of tranquilizers, the temptation exists (more in this specialty than in some of the others) to abuse drugs.

PROFESSIONAL ORGANIZATION
American Psychiatric Association
1400 K Street NW
Washington, DC 20005

BOARD OF CERTIFICATION
American Board of Psychiatry and Neurology, Inc.
500 Lake Cook Road
Deerfield, IL 60015

10

The Anesthesiologist

SALARY
$140,000–$200,000 ($160,000 is the national average)

YEARS OF RESIDENCY
4 years of residency training in anesthesiology

DESCRIPTION OF JOB
If you ever had an operation, the anesthesiologist was the doctor who stationed himself near your head during the surgery, next to all the machines and typically out of sight. You probably met him the night before the scheduled operation, when he stopped by to ask you a few more medical questions and to explain his part in the surgery. You might not remember his face, but you'll recall his voice because it's often the last thing you hear before falling unconscious. He's the one who asks you to count backwards from 100 (if he's using general anesthesia for the operation). Because your sense of hearing is the last sense to leave you, you may drift off with his voice in your ear. He is also the one to rouse you from unconsciousness, calling your name, and asking you how you feel. Although the surgeon is the one to perform the operation, the anesthesiologist is the one to keep you comfortable—and alive—throughout.

The anesthesiologist administers different types of anesthesia (and analgesia) during an operation. Sometimes he renders a person unconscious, sometimes only blocking sensation (as with an epidural injection, for example). He or she has to know a great deal about each patient to deliver the appropriate dosage of anesthesia. That's why he talks to the patient before each elective surgery, and thoroughly familiarizes himself with that patient's chart. During the operation, the anesthesiologist focuses his attention on the patient and her vital signs. Not only does he have to make sure the patient is sufficiently comfortable, but also tolerating the surgery. He alerts the surgeon if the patient's vital signs deteriorate, and in the event of heart failure assists the doctors with resuscitation.

Aside from general anesthesia, the anesthesiologist needs to know how to inject analgesics into the "epidural space" of the spinal cord, in the small of the back. Women in labor commonly request the epidural block because it relieves them of pain without the accompanying sense of dead weight. Great skill is needed to give this shot properly; it is uncomfortable for the patient, who must lie curled up in the fetal position while the shot is being administered. If the anesthesiologist accidentally hits the spinal cord, he risks paralying the patient in the process.

During the operation (or progression of labor), the anesthesiologist continually checks to make sure the patient is properly sedated. If the surgeon operates for six to eight hours, the anesthesiologist is right there with him. When the surgeon indicates the operation is finished, the anesthesiologist brings the patient back to consciousness, and later stops by to check for any ill effects.

Anesthesiologists need to be on call, too. A group practice allows them to share the on-call duties so that one gets an evening or so a week at home without the threat of being paged.

QUALITIES NEEDED

Here is another specialty in which you don't have to have a great bedside manner. If you tend to be shy, you can still be a good anesthesiologist. Patients may choose their anesthesiologist for an elective surgical procedure, but usually they end up with the person the surgeon recommends. Because you'll form more of a relationship with the surgeon with whom you work, it's more important to get along well with your colleagues. Being knowledgable, confident, and unflappable are more highly valued than sociability.

Good communication skills will help you explain your procedure to the patients.

You'll need stamina to get through the longer operations, the ability to think clearly in an emergency, and the resourcefulness to save a patient who is reacting to the anesthesia. The anesthesiologist needs to be obsessive about detail, focused, and self-confident. A sense of humor helps counterbalance the stress of the job.

ADVANTAGES

You are well reimbursed for the job that you perform. Anesthesiologists typically make high salaries because these are the very procedures that insurance companies reimburse best. You'll enjoy the respect of your community and your medical colleagues (if you work well with them).

Your work will be challenging and varied, and if you like the technical end of medicine better than working directly with patients, you'll find this specialty rewarding. Your hours can be set (with the exception of on-call emergencies), and job opportunities abound both in hospital settings and the military.

And don't think you won't be appreciated. Many women facing painful labor will love you almost as much as their obstetrician. Their obstetrician may deliver the baby, but you'll make the experience *comfortable*.

DISADVANTAGES

If you like working with patients, you may be frustrated by this specialty because there are few opportunities for ongoing contact.

Because anesthesiology is one of the higher-risk specialties, malpractice insurance rates are high. An error in this specialty could result in permanent paralysis or brain death. Successful malpractice suits would compromise your standing in the profession, not to mention raise your rates. Vindication is a small victory, at best; the public remembers the allegations much longer than they do the positive outcome.

Making a mistake that either hurts or kills a patient is a heavy burden. A malpractice suit may be the least of your worries; knowing that you've hurt someone may be harder to live with. It's distressing to lose a patient during an operation even if it happens through no fault of your own.

Because the hours can be demanding at times (and your responsibilities are so great), anesthesiologists often burn out from all the stress. Having such ready access to drugs sometimes propels them into drug abuse. In fact, anesthesiologists (as a group) are the most likely of the doctors to abuse drugs and alcohol.

PROFESSIONAL ORGANIZATION

American Society of Anesthesiologists
520 North Northwest Highway
Park Ridge, IL 60068-2573

BOARD OF CERTIFICATION
The American Board of Anesthesiology
100 Constitution Plaza
Hartford, CT 06103-1796
(No requirement for recertification.)

11

The Obstetrician/Gynecologist

SALARY
$150,000–$230,000 (Balance these salaries against very high malpractice insurance premiums—around $50,000 a year.)

YEARS OF RESIDENCY
4 years in obstetrics/gynecology

or

1 year in internal medicine

and

3 years in obstetrics/gynecology

DESCRIPTION OF JOB
When you think of this specialty, you probably think of someone who delivers babies. Actually, that is only part of the job of the obstetrician/gynecologist. She also diag-

noses and treats abnormal vaginal bleeding; cervical, ovarian, and endometrial cancer; infertility, amenorrhea (absence of menstrual periods); venereal diseases, pelvic infections, and some bladder problems. Because of high malpractice rates, some doctors prefer not to practice their obstetric skills. There are certainly enough women needing Pap smears and pelvic exams, birth control information, and treatment of infections that the gynecologist need not lack for patients.

The doctor who does choose to deliver babies will have a booming practice, though, because the number of obstetricians has declined in recent years. And women will continue to have babies. So, let's look at what an obstetrician does.

She delivers babies, of course, but that's really just a small part of what she does. She might do a fertility workup on a woman who is having trouble conceiving a child. If the problem turns out to be scarred fallopian tubes because of an earlier pelvic infection, she may have to operate to clear the tubes. If it turns out the woman isn't ovulating, the obstetrician may prescribe fertility drugs to stimulate ovulation. Once the woman does become pregnant, the obstetrician's work has only begun. She continues to see her patient monthly, measuring the circumference of the woman's belly as she progresses, and listening to the baby's heartbeat. She orders bloodwork to determine the Rh factor, anemia, and the possibility of venereal disease—including AIDS. She may order an ultrasound of the fetus (sound waves bouncing off the mother's belly clearly depict the fetus in the uterus) to determine any obvious defects. If the patient has a healthy pregnancy, the obstetrician need only check her monthly and provide emotional support. If the patient experiences heavy bleeding during the pregnancy, the doctor worries about placental problems or a threatened miscarriage. She may have to treat the patient for toxemia or gestational diabetes, both high-risk situations. During the pregnancy, she also treats minor sore throats and cold symptoms, since the patient is already coming to see her each month.

Ultimately, the obstetrician prepares to deliver the baby. If the baby has turned and is engaged in the pelvis in the normal headdown position, the woman will probably have a vaginal delivery. The obstetrician (or the one who is on call that day) monitors the patient's labor, checking on her periodically. When she is ready to deliver, the obstetrician takes her to the delivery room. If the baby is in a complicated breech presentation (buttocks or feet first), or in the event of an emergency (meconium-stained amniotic fluid or fetal distress), the obstetrician will perform a caesarean section. The obstetrician, then, is actually a surgeon. And because she has surgical skills, she (not the pediatrician) may perform the circumcision later if the child is a boy.

Since women have babies at all hours of the day and night, an obstetrician's schedule is unpredictable. Some caesareans can be scheduled ahead of time, but otherwise, deliveries occur at random. Most obstetricians share on-call with other doctors so that they can get a decent night's sleep once in a while.

A typical day for an obstetrician might start out with the obstetrician checking on her hospitalized patients (those recovering from hysterectomies as well as the ones who've just given birth). After writing orders for medication and discharge, she heads to her office (which she may share with several other obstetricians) to see private patients throughout the day. If she's on call that day, nurses may interrupt her appointments to tell her she's needed at the hospital. After 5:00, she may swing by the hospital on her way home to check on her patients. And of course, if she's on call, she probably won't get to sleep through the night.

QUALITIES NEEDED

Above everything else, the obstetrician needs to like women. The sensitive physician would realize, for example, that a cold speculum (used in the pelvic exam) is jarring. She'd think to warm it in hot water before using it. She wouldn't minimize the concerns of a mother-to-be, chiding her for being slightly hysterical, and she wouldn't resent the phone calls in the middle of the night.

If you're thinking of this specialty, you'll need energy (for the demanding hours), manual dexterity for the surgical procedures, and resourcefulness (for when things don't go according to plan). You'll also need good listening skills, a keen eye for detail, and a sense of humor (to keep it all in perspective). Women in labor run the gamut of emotions, and though you'll be their hero when it's all over, you might not be so popular when they're hurting. It helps if you can take the good and bad in stride.

Because so many malpractice suits are filed against these doctors, you're well advised to stay on top of the paperwork. Documentation could save your practice.

ADVANTAGES

This specialty has many advantages although they're offset by some serious disadvantages cited in the next section. For one thing, the work is challenging, gratifying, and financially rewarding. For another, bringing babies into the world is joyful work. Women will love you because you've made it possible.

You'll also enjoy the respect of your community.

The opportunities to practice this specialty are endless, in part because obstetricians are giving up their practice because of high insurance premiums. And remember: women are always having babies.

If you're female, bear in mind there's a growing need for women obstetricians, especially in HMOs, where the hours may be more normal than most.

DISADVANTAGES

Now, here's the downside. Malpractice insurance premiums are skyhigh for a very good reason. People don't like it when they think they've received poor treatment; they *especially* don't like it when something is wrong with their baby. Though it may not have a thing to do with your handling of the case, if something is wrong with their baby at birth, they're going to want to blame someone. Suing the doctor sometimes makes a person feel he's at least *doing something* about the situation.

Malpractice suits are costly (no matter what the outcome); if you lose, your rates go up, and your reputation is tarnished. If you win, your rates probably still go up, and few people note that you were cleared of the charges. . . .

Delivering babies is joyful work . . . most of the time. Some babies are stillborn; others are born with severe defects and die shortly after birth. If you're not used to loss, you'll find this work occasionally unbearable. Losing a patient is painful, but losing a baby is a hundred times worse. Babies are not supposed to die before they've had a chance to live, and they're not supposed to be born suffering. If you can't keep some emotional distance from your patients, you'll be overwhelmed by each bad outcome.

Obstetrics is a high-stress job with unpredictable hours. It is another specialty with the potential for drug abuse. Since many doctors resort to pills to help them stay awake for deliveries, and then pills to help them get to sleep, it's easy to see how they can end up addicted to a string of medications.

Your homelife is affected by the demands of the job.

It's hard to be emotionally available to your loved ones when you're not physically available.

And finally, like any surgeon, you always risk exposure to AIDS.

BOARD OF CERTIFICATION
The American Board of Obstetrics and Gynecology, Inc.
936 North 34th Street
Seattle, WA 98103

(Certificates are valid for ten years. At the end of that time, the candidate must submit to further examination for recertification.)

12

The Pediatrician

SALARY
$90,000–$120,000

YEARS OF RESIDENCY
3 years of residency in pediatrics

DESCRIPTION OF JOB
Pediatricians, by definition, provide care to children, from newborns through the age of seventeen. They treat common childhood infections, immunize children against diseases, and treat minor injuries and burns. They also treat more serious conditions such as asthma, diabetes, cystic fibrosis, and cancer. Pediatricians work in clinics associated with hospitals, have solo practices and group practices. Women choose this specialty over others, in part because they can control the hours (through part-time practices and salaried positions).

Let's examine some typical experiences of the pediatrician. If he's accepting new clients, he may get a call from prospective parents when the woman is still pregnant. She and her husband are probably "shopping around" for a pediatrician. They'll meet with him to assess his skill and bedside manner; he'll go over his responsibilities and theirs, as parents of a newborn. If they agree to use him as their child's doctor, he'll be called when the woman is in labor and ready to deliver. In the event of complications, a pediatrician attends the birth (if he can make it; otherwise the pediatric resident on duty will stand in for him, and the attending doctor will appear thereafter.) The pediatrician will check out the newborn and if she appears healthy admit her to the regular nursery. If the baby is born prematurely or has signs of heart damage or respiratory distress, he'll admit her to a specialized unit for more intensive care. If the obstetrician knows that the baby has passed meconium (had a bowel movement in utero, where the danger is that she could aspirate parts), he alerts the pediatrician, who'll stand by to suction the baby upon delivery.

The pediatrician continues to be responsible for the newborn in the hospital, while the obstetrician cares for the mother. If he's sensitive to the mother's needs (especially the first-time mother), he'll spend time with her as well discussing the infant's needs.

Following discharge, the pediatrician remains the baby's primary doctor. He'll see the baby at regular intervals (growing farther apart, as she ages) to make sure she is doing well and to immunize her against life-threatening illnesses. He also looks for signs of abuse and will report such to the appropriate agencies. He'll no doubt hear from distraught parents when the baby has a fever or cries continuously. He can treat bacterial infections with antibiotics, fever with acetaminophen, and distraught parents with emotional support. Many new mothers call the doctor frequently just to learn if their baby is "normal."

Some children are born with terminal conditions, such as cystic fibrosis and AIDS. Others develop life-threatening conditions such as asthma, juvenile diabetes, and cancer. One of the hardest parts of the pediatrician's job is to help these young patients for as long as they have. Watching children die, knowing there is little you can do to delay death, is heart-rending work, but not all of your patients will live to adulthood. Your job is to reduce their suffering and to keep up their spirits. While you don't have to get along with the parents, it helps if you can cultivate a relationship with them as well.

Children have a lot of accidents; you'll probably see your share of sprained and fractured limbs, as well as accidental poisonings. Infants and toddlers swallow the most unimaginable things—bottlecaps, iron pills (which incidentally are very dangerous to kids), and funny-tasting room deodorizers shaped like mushrooms. They also burn their fingers playing with matches, and poke each other with scissors. Left unattended in bathtubs, they almost drown. The pediatrician deals with a lot of emergencies, which is part of the reason he gets behind schedule in his private practice.

A typical day can take him from the hospital to his office and back to the hospital again at night. His patients may include an ailing newborn, a toddler whose mother may be burning him with cigarettes, an adolescent who needs a physical okay to play sports, and a ten-year-old just diagnosed with leukemia. The pediatrician will consult other specialists and coordinate cancer treatment; he may get tied up filling out reports for DHS (Department of Human Services) and explaining himself to then angry parents. Not all of a pediatrician's day is spent with children. . . .

QUALITIES NEEDED

Above anything else, the pediatrician needs to *love children.* If you can't stand little kids with runny noses, you're looking at the wrong specialty. If you don't like noisy waiting rooms or screaming babies, you're in over

75

your head. If you genuinely like kids, you'll find this work joyful and rewarding. It's nice, too, if you can get along well with the kids' parents, but it's not mandatory. Some people will still retain a pediatrician (despite a prickly disposition) if their kids like him.

You need courage (and good communication skills) to confront caregivers about abuse. You need sensitivity, so you don't end up patronizing kids. They can always spot someone talking down to them and won't listen to you after that. To develop sensitivity, you mostly need good listening skills.

Naturally, like anyone working with children, you need patience and resourcefulness. If a child balks at getting a shot, it's better to seek his cooperation than to simply overpower him. And with all the paperwork that goes along with the job, you're well-advised to stay on top of this detail. . . .

ADVANTAGES

Pediatrics is a good specialty for women who like children and want some control over their hours. HMOs offer salaried positions and job incentives to attract pediatricians. The work is challenging and mostly rewarding. (Kids are very upfront with their opinions; either they'll cry when they see you, or give you a bearhug.)

Malpractice insurance premiums are the lowest of the specialties. You still face the threat of a malpractice suit, just as any doctor does, but obviously the chances are less than in other specialties.

You have the opportunity to develop a lengthy relationship with a family. If it appeals to you, you'll get to see these babies grow into adults. You're well appreciated, have high status in your community, and though you're paid less than some other doctors, it's certainly an above-average salary.

DISADVANTAGES

The downside to this specialty is the threat of a malpractice suit (which exists with any medical career) and the number of hours worked. Pediatricians can put in enormous hours between the hospital and the office, especially if they don't share their on-call duties with many others. It's hard to bring up a family—to be there for them—when you're needed at the office.

The lower salary reflects the type of reimbursable services you offer. As you may have noticed with your family physican and internist, office visits are reimbursed at a lower rate than technical procedures.

Some of pediatrics is depressing work. To some, there's little reward to working with a terminally ill patient, especially a child. If you get too attached to these patients, you'll be overwhelmed by their suffering and eventual death. To keep perspective, you have to accept that the real enemy is not death, but suffering. Somtimes, the pediatrician can delay a patient's dying, but he can't prevent it altogether. And to paraphrase Stewart Alsop, at some point a dying person needs to die, just as a tired person needs to sleep. What the pediatrician can try to do is make the patient comfortable. If you aren't comfortable treating children who could die, you won't be able to handle this job.

You'll no doubt struggle with some ethical dilemmas: do you administer morphine to a child in pain, thereby hastening the child's death, or do you let her live awhile longer, albeit in great pain? What do you do for a baby born too early to survive? How many times will you resuscitate him before you let him die. How will you feel if you aggressively treat an infant who survives but is severely damaged despite (or because of) your interventions?

Finally, the paperwork (as in most professions) is

staggering. Keeping up with progress notes is hard enough, but filing abuse reports is daunting.

PROFESSIONAL ORGANIZATION
American Academy of Pediatrics
141 Northwest Point Boulevard
Elk Grove Village, IL 60009-0927

BOARD OF CERTIFICATION
The American Board of Pediatrics
111 Silver Cedar Court
Chapel Hill, NC 27514-1651
(Certificates are good for seven years.)

13

The Radiologist

SALARY
$150,000–$250,000 (The high salaries reflect the better rate of reimbursement for technical procedures.)

YEARS OF RESIDENCY
4 years of residency training in radiology

The radiology oncologist spends 1 year in internal medicine, 3 to 4 years in radiation oncology

DESCRIPTION OF JOB
If you've ever needed an x-ray, you've run into someone from the radiology department. While many technicians actually perform the x-rays, the radiologist heads the department and oversees their work. For some of the more difficult procedures, he either supervises his technicians' efforts or performs the job himself. (We'll look at the various procedures in a minute.) The radiologist has been called a "doctor's doctor" because his job is to help other doctors with their diagnosis.

The radiation oncologist provides radiation treatment

to people with cancer in order to shrink or destroy tumors.

Let's look at some of the tools of his trade. No doubt the most commonly recognized machine is the x-ray. People get x-rays for everything: chest x-rays to detect tuberculosis, x-rays to determine broken bones, and more elaborate barium studies to determine problems in the gastrointestinal tract. Not only does the radiologist have to know how to position the patient and run the machine, but he needs to know how to read the pictures afterwards. He may do a bone scan to determine any abnormal areas in the skeleton. To do a pyelogram, he'll inject contrast material into a vein to reach the kidney quickly. The condition of the kidney (as well as urinary tract) is clearly outlined as the material proceeds to excretion. A cholecystrogram, in a similar process, provides a detailed picture of the gallbladder; a myelogram does the same for the spinal cord and branching nerves. He may do a CAT scan, which makes a computerized picture of the part of the body examined. The scanner takes pictures (in diagonal slices) as it moves over the body, and then puts them together to form a three-dimensional picture. These pictures give the surgeon a clearer image of a possible tumor. Although expensive, CAT scans have greatly reduced the number of exploratory surgeries being done today. MRI (magnetic resonance imaging) machines have improved on the CAT scanner's abilities. A more commonly used machine is the ultrasound, which is used to image the breast (as a supplement to mammograms), to study tumors and cysts, the gallbladder itself, the heart and kidneys. And of course, it's used in obstetrics to image the fetus, providing all sorts of information. For example, the radiologist can determine any structural defects of the fetus, the sex of the unborn baby (if he has a clear view of the genitals), the likely due date, a good estimate of the baby's weight, whether or not the fetus is growing properly, and the position of the placenta. If the obstetrician needs to perform amniocentesis, an ultrasound image of the uterus will help him better position the needle.

Anytime a doctor is uncertain about a diagnosis, he consults the radiologist. Before anyone undergoes surgery, he'll see the radiologist for x-rays and other imagings. As technologies improve, the radiologist becomes even better at making an accurate diagnosis. The demand for his services in the future will only increase.

QUALITIES NEEDED

The radiologist obviously needs a keen eye for detail. Erring in a diagnosis can have fatal consequences, particularly when talking about a tumor. He needs to be assertive (when dealing with other doctors who may be tempted to prioritize their orders) and courteous (since he relies on other doctors to furnish him his patients). Although it's not necessary to have a good bedside manner because of his limited contact with patients, it encourages more cooperation if he does. He needs to be sensitive to the concerns of his cancer patients, who are probably scared to death of suffering and humiliated by their appearance.

Since he runs a department, he needs to be attentive to his technicians (to make sure they do a good job) and attentive to the paperwork that is generated in this specialty.

ADVANTAGES

Radiology is another high-paying specialty because of the better reimbursement for diagnostic procedures. The work is challenging and varied, with the added opportunity to teach and do research on the side.

Radiologists occupy positions of power in the medical

community. Even surgeons—the most active of the "doers" in this profession—can't make a move without consulting them.

While working with cancer patients can be depressing at times, helping to cure them of the disease *is* rewarding. Likewise, helping prospective parents visualize their babies with ultrasound can be a joyful event.

The radiologists' hours are more regular than in most professions, and job opportunities abound in both hospital settings and private practice. Obviously, a reason to work for a hospital is that the high cost of buying and maintaining the equipment is not your responsibility.

DISADVANTAGES

If you prefer working with patients, you'll be disappointed in this specialty because the opportunity to develop relationships is not there. Most patients don't pick their radiologist; their doctor recommends one.

Day in and day out, you're around radioactive materials, and though you handle them carefully, they're still dangerous. If you're a woman who is considering getting pregnant, you might want to find a less challenging environment.

An unpleasant aspect of this job is tangling with other doctors who demand that you rush through their requests. If you're unassertive to begin with, you'll find yourself working overtime just to handle everything you promised in a hurry.

Running a department means taking responsibility for the work your subordinates do. If you're not good at delegating tasks or confronting people about the quality of their work, you'll have to do all the procedures yourself—which would become a 24-hour-a-day job.

Working with cancer patients can be depressing at

times, especially when you've done all you can to help and it just isn't enough.

Finally, as in all the medical specialties these days, you have to worry about whether a disgruntled patient (or her family) will find fault with your procedures and file suit. Malpractice suits are costly (because whether you win or lose, your insurance premiums will probably go up) and of course damaging to your reputation.

PROFESSIONAL ORGANIZATIONS
American College of Radiology
1891 Preston White Drive
Reston, VA 22091

American College of Nuclear Physicians
1101 Connecticut Avenue NW
Washington, DC 20036

BOARD OF CERTIFICATION
American Board of Radiology
2301 West Big Beaver Road
Troy, MI 48084

The Pathologist and Medical Examiner

SALARY
$100,000–$150,000 (national average around $125,000.)

YEARS OF RESIDENCY
Anatomic and clinical pathologist—5 years combined training in anatomic and clinical pathology

Anatomic pathologist—4 years training in anatomic pathology

Clinical pathologist—4 years training in clinical pathology

DESCRIPTION OF JOB
Pathologists are directors of laboratories (in either hospitals or private settings) who specialize in anatomic pathology, clinical pathology, or both. Sometimes, the two overlap, but as a rule, the anatomic pathologist studies structural changes in tissues, whereas the clinical pathologist studies the chemical and structural changes in body fluids and tissues.

If you've ever had blood drawn and analyzed, you can credit a pathologist. If you've ever had a growth removed in surgery, you can credit the pathologist with

84

determining its status (malignant or benign). If you wonder who determines what kind of infection you have and what drug will kill it, credit the pathologist again.

If you have watched reruns of "Quincy, M.D.", you probably think of a pathologist as an older man who works in the cold basement of a hospital performing autopsies on people who died suspicious deaths. Actually, pathologists are almost as likely to be women who practice their skills in bright, cheerful laboratories. This is a good specialty for women because of the more regular hours and the opportunities to interact with their colleagues.

Pathologists examine and diagnose all tissue removed during surgery. When a biopsy is made of a lump in the breast, for example, the pathologist is the one who determines if the growth is malignant or benign. Based on her assessment, the surgeon then either performs radical surgery or merely excises the lump. The consequences are great, so the pathologist cannot afford to make mistakes. She examines routine Pap smears to detect cancer in its earliest stages; she examines blood (for infections, including HIV), and cultures stool samples and urine and sputum samples. Once she determines the presence of microorganisms, she often recommends the best drug to combat them.

The pathologist does perform autopsies to determine cause of death (especially if a doctor's judgment is in question). The forensic pathologist serves as the coroner (or medical examiner) whose job is to investigate "sudden, unexpected, suspicious, and violent death." Her determination of the cause of death is usually the final word on the subject.

Pathologists make good teachers and researchers. They've been crucial in the battle to find a cure for AIDS, developing and testing an assortment of drugs. They have been instrumental in diagnosing and suggesting treatment for environmentally induced disease. The pathologist, then, can be considered both a super sleuth and scientist rolled into one.

QUALITIES NEEDED

If you're intriqued by this medical specialty, you'll need a keen eye for detail, seriousness of purpose, and attention to paperwork. Every other doctor in the medical community (not to mention the police) consult your expertise; shoddy work will damage your reputation, not to mention affect people's lives.

You must be able to perform well under pressure. Even though you're in a less visible position, your contribution to patient care is crucial. If you're a medical examiner, you'll no doubt have to testify in court, defending your opinion against lawyers whose job will be to challenge you. Naturally, you'll need a high degree of self-confidence (and courage to stand by your convictions).

Patience and persistence will enable you to keep at your research and to note all possibilities for a patient's death, not just the most obvious one.

Since you're responsible for the smooth running of your department, it helps to have effective supervisory skills. You don't necessarily have to be charming (or possess a good bedside manner) since you won't have any patient contact, but you will need good communication skills to work with your colleagues.

Since part of your job may be working with contaminated blood products, you need to be a cautious person. If you're squeamish about cadavers, you won't last long in this specialty. You'll have to perform an autopsy sometime. It helps if you have a sense of humor to keep things in perspective. Dealing with pathology (and death) as you do, you might need to find something to laugh at from time to time. If you're too serious all the time, you might find yourself overwhelmed by the intensity of your labors.

ADVANTAGES

Determining disease and recommending treatment are challenging work, not to mention gratifying. You're well paid, and you're a highly valued member of the medical team. Your word is final.

You get to practice in a quiet setting (versus the hustle and bustle of the emergency room or the pediatric clinic), and your hours are more regular than in most specialties. (In fact, the residency hours are less demanding, on average, as well.) Pathology is a good field for women (not only for the above reasons, but because they are treated more as equals in this specialty).

Opportunities abound for pathologists. Some 75 percent work in hospitals, but others (more and more successfully because of the increase in ambulatory care these days) practice in private labs. Others work in the military and in state and local governments. Along with the opportunity to practice anywhere is the chance to combine research and teaching with your job.

An advantage to working in a lab, not providing treatment to patients, is that if you diagnose a malignancy, you need not get emotionally involved with the patient. He or she remains only a name to you.

Finally, pathologists do not face many of the ethical dilemmas faced by doctors who provide direct patient care. They don't have to worry about resuscitating a dying patient or "pulling the plug" on a person who has been declared brain dead.

DISADVANTAGES

This specialty is not for the squeamish. If you object to working with blood and analyzing sputum and stool samples, you won't be able to stand this work.

Having the "final word" on a diagnosis can be a burden as well as an honor. If you make a mistake, the result can sometimes be fatal. Calling a growth benign when it's really malignant obviously jeopardizes the patient's chances for full recovery (when the malignancy is discovered later). Such high stress on the job can lead to burnout.

Because you work with contaminated blood products, you run the risk of contracting disease yourself—the most serious being AIDS, of course.

If you like working with patients, you'll be dissatisfied because there are few opportunities to interact with them. On the other hand, if you don't want notoriety, you shouldn't accept the state medical examiner's position. The public will know who you are. Coroners get a lot of press for the obvious reasons—they're continually dealing with suspicious or violent deaths. If you prefer to work in out-of-the-way settings, a government job is not for you.

As in any medical specialty, the potential exists for a law suit. About the only things you can do are to insure yourself adequately and practice good medicine.

Finally, the paperwork is endless. Given the importance of your determinations, you can't let the documentation slide.

PROFESSIONAL ORGANIZATION
American Association of Pathologists
9650 Rockville Pike
Bethesda, MD 20814

College of American Pathologists
325 Waukegan Road
Northfield, IL 60093

Intersociety Committee on Pathology Information, Inc.
4733 Bethesda Avenue
Bethesda, MD 20014

BOARD OF CERTIFICATION
The American Board of Pathology
5401 West Kennedy Boulevard
Tampa, FL 33622-5915

15

The Dermatologist

SALARY

$100,000–$200,000 (The national average appears to be $150,000.)

YEARS OF RESIDENCY

1 year in internal medicine, plus

3 years in dermatology

DESCRIPTION OF JOB

The dermatologist treats "diseases and ailments" of the skin, hair, nails, and mucous membranes. He may remove scars, perform hair transplants, and treat various conditions: dermatitis, eczema, urticaria (hives), psoriasis, scabies, warts, the common cold sore (or fever blister), skin cancers, and adverse reactions to medications.

The dermatologist has trained under close supervision in a number of areas including skin pathology, bacteriology, allergy and immunology, radiology, and surgery. If a person consults him for a sudden outbreak of hives, the dermatologist would need to discern an allergic reaction (to food or medications) from a case of "bad nerves." If he diagnoses a skin cancer, he possesses the surgical skills to remove it.

Dermatologists can treat some rather bizarre skin conditions, as evidenced by Michael Jackson's revelation that he is being treated for vitiligo. This is a skin disorder that eventually leaves a person with splotchy patches of whitened skin. While the dermatologists can't replace the pigment—melanin—that's lost, they can even out the discoloration with makeup.

Other doctors routinely consult the dermatologist when a diagnosis eludes them. Often, the dermatologist is skilled enough to determine the cause of a skin condition by physical examination alone. (Sometimes, patients gripe that he didn't do a thing except "look at the spots." Dermatologists can culture a skin eruption, but usually it is not necessary and only adds to the patient's expense. People are paying for his knowledge, as much as his time.)

The dermatologist takes samples and either sends them to the lab for analysis or does the work himself. He may prescribe x-rays and ultraviolet light treatments for certain conditions. At times he fulfills the roles of pathologist, radiologist, and researcher.

The dermatologist typically has a solo practice, though increasing numbers are practicing in groups. He usually sees patients in his office, mostly referred from other doctors. He also sees patients in the hospital, but most of his work takes place during regular office hours. (Which is one of the good things about this specialty: You can actually have a decent homelife.)

As long as patients continue to expose themselves to the sun's harmful rays and environmental hazards, as long as teenagers grapple with acne, and people react to mold spores in the air, the dermatologist will always have a job.

QUALITIES NEEDED

Like any doctor involved in diagnostic work, you'll need a keen eye and the patience to find the cure. You'll need to be knowledgable because the skin affects (and is affected by) other parts of the body. You need manual dexterity for surgery, and good communication skills to convey your treatment regime to patients.

This is one specialty where you need to be pleasant and approachable. Your reputation depends on your patients' satisfaction. If you have a prickly disposition, they may trade you in. Patients with skin disorders (and fears about cancer) feel particularly vulnerable. The problems they have are visible to everyone they encounter. Adolescence can be a crummy time anyway, what with raging hormones embarrassing you at every opportunity. Imagine how demoralizing it is to have a face full of pimples, or arms and legs crusty from eczema. In each case, the dermatologist has to put these young patients at ease, being sensitive to their embarrassment and desire for an instant cure.

He needs to be thorough (so as not to miss key symptoms), disciplined (since he won't have someone standing over him telling him what to do each day), and resourceful (for often, disease can mimic a variety of skin conditions).

ADVANTAGES

This specialty has many advantages: dermatologists are well paid, and opportunities for practice (which abound at the present) will only increase in the near future.

The hours are more regular than in some specialties, enabling these doctors to lead more satisfactory lives at home.

The work is challenging, and varied, and you get to play different roles (pathologist, radiologist, and immunologist) to some degree. You have the best of all worlds: direct patient contact, consultations with your colleagues, and quiet hours spent in the lab.

And topping it all off are reasonable malpractice insurance rates.

DISADVANTAGES

Although you do have some direct patient contact, it's not the same kind of on-going relationship that you'd have with patients as a family physician or internist. Skin conditions clear up, and patients no longer need your services. As a dermatologist, you don't tend to follow a person through the course of his lifetime—only for the duration of his skin problems.

Since the dermatologist relies heavily on referrals, his start-up in private practice may be slow. You have to build up a reputation, and that takes time. Since you're not a primary-care physician, you won't be the type of doctor that people routinely look up in the Yellow Pages. Most people bring their problems—even their skin conditions—to their internist or family physician first. It's then up to him or her to refer the patient to you for more specialized work.

If you have your own private practice, you'll need to spend a lot of money on office equipment and lab supplies.

Because you are sometimes working with contagious viral conditions (and unpleasant bouts of scabies), you run the risk of catching these yourself. Though you don't "catch" melanomas, you can get AIDS from an infected person (whose body fluids accidentally come into contact with yours).

And as in any medical practice, you run the risk of a malpractice suit. However, since insurance premiums are low, the likelihood of a suit is less than in other specialties.

PROFESSIONAL ORGANIZATION
American Academy of Dermatology
P.O. Box 4014
Schaumburg, IL 60168-4014

BOARD OF CERTIFICATION
American Board of Dermatology
Henry Ford Hospital
Detroit, MI 48202
(Certificates are valid for ten years.)

16

The Emergency Room Physician

SALARY

$100,000–$175,000 (The amount is similar whether you work in a salaried position or "fee for service".)

YEARS OF RESIDENCY

3 years in emergency medicine training

DESCRIPTION OF JOB

It's hard to imagine a specialty with more excitement and challenges than this one. The emergency room doctor deals with every case that walks through the hospital's doors; obviously, that requires an enormous amount of skill and the ability to make life and death decisions quickly.

Some hospitals, called trauma centers, specialize in the treatment of injuries and gunshot wounds. Some inner-city hospitals see both people who can and can't pay for treatment, which means they probably see transients as well as those with insurance coverage. Emergency room doctors are prepared to deal with everything.

Naturally, they've seen their share of broken bones

and kids who've swallowed the contents of the medicine cabinet. They've stabilized heart attack and stroke victims before admitting them for observation. They've sutured wounds and controlled the bleeding of trauma victims before sending the latter off to surgery. They've treated people who can't breathe because of asthma or an allergic reaction (to something they ate or touched).

Accidents will always keep the emergency room doctor in business. Toddlers pull things down on themselves, bump their heads, and fall on heating grates. Elderly people fall down stairs or roll out of bed, and everyone falls on the ice at one time or another. Dogs will always bite, and cats will always scratch.

Teenagers, who consider themselves immortal, take too many risks; they sometimes drive too fast and fool around with drugs. People drink and drive, despite good sense and fines if they get caught.

One of the least pleasant tasks for the emergency room doctor is discovering abuse. Kids come in with bruises all the time. Naturally, their parents claim they fell down, but sometimes the pattern of bruises isn't consistent with a fall. Sometimes it really looks more like a beating. Kids come in scalded, and the parents say they turned the hot water on themselves in the tub. An elderly woman complains that her children hit her when she doesn't eat, and she has bruises all over her back and arms. In these cases, it's not enough just to treat the wounds; the physician is also obligated to report his suspicions and to keep the patient in the hospital until the proper authorities can take over.

People have nervous breakdowns; they quit eating; they think they're God; they threaten their neighbors. Sometimes, physical disease makes people psychotic (out of touch with reality). When their behavior intrudes on other people, they wind up at the hospital. It's then the emergency room doctor's job to decide if the person is hallucinating from a psychiatric disorder or a physical disease. And to treat or refer.

Alcoholics come to the emergency room at predictable intervals because the drinking is destroying their livers. AIDS patients come in with recurrent bouts of pneumonia, and anorexic young women are brought in for not eating.

The emergency room doctor, then, sees every crisis imaginable, stabilizes most of them (inappropriate admissions are referred elsewhere), and either sends them home or admits for observation or surgery. For obvious reasons, these doctors practice in a hospital, usually as salaried employees (though they can be paid "fee for service"). Many emergency rooms employ some doctors (still in residency training), who are "moonlighting" (under supervision) on the weekends or the weeknights they're not on call. As you can well imagine, there are lots of opportunities for these energetic young doctors. And older emergency room physicians can move into administrative positions, if they're so inclined.

QUALITIES NEEDED

Because you're always dealing with emergencies (as opposed to scheduled office visits), you have to be able to think quickly (and effectively) on your feet. You need to be decisive and self-confident, which may make you seem arrogant to others. Like the surgeon, arrogance (in the form of conceit) will keep you confident, able to make those life and death decisions.

You'll need energy and enthusiasm to survive the sometimes frantic pace. Some say emergency room physicians should be young, but energy really knows no age. You just have to like (or be able to tolerate) a chaotic environment and a lot of demands on your skill.

It helps if you don't panic easily. Sometimes, if you can just **give the impression** that you're calm, your patients will relax, as well. Your staff will, no doubt, handle the chaos better if you set a good example.

A good bedside manner is not a prerequisite for this specialty, because most people would rather have a skilled doctor than a charming one. But, of course, it would be even better to get **both**. . . . Being friendly and empathetic puts the patient more at ease. Nobody wants to be treated by a doctor who acts as if your emergency is spoiling his day.

You also need to be direct when you confront people about abuse. You can't let a child return home where the next beating might kill him.

Finally, you could probably use a good sense of humor. The stress in this type of work can lead to cynicism and burnout; it helps to find things to laugh at so you don't take yourself too seriously. Naturally, you have to take your responsibilities seriously, but you don't want them to get you down in the process.

ADVANTAGES

As mentioned earlier, you'll be hard pressed to find more exciting, challenging work. Your day is never scheduled, and your patients come in all shapes and sizes, experiencing a whole range of problems. Nobody's ever gotten bored in this specialty.

Opportunities abound for emergency room physicians, and you'll never run out of patients.

Saving people's lives is gratifying work. Resuscitating someone who's had a heart attack, bringing back the person who was dying from smoke inhalation, successfully pumping the stomach of a child who ate his mother's vitamins—these are achievements that make all the work seem worthwhile.

As medical specialties go, this one is relatively high-paying. You get to develop ties with other physicians (with whom you need to consult on some cases).

Not having on-going relationships with patients can often be an advantage, since it keeps you from getting emotionally involved in the cases. It's especially a blessing in abuse situations, where you don't have to continue to monitor the family situation.

Working in a hospital, there are no start-up costs or referral sources to woo. And if you decide to move on to another specialty (when your enthusiasm wanes), you'll already have a broad base of knowledge and skills to draw upon.

DISADVANTAGES

While emergency medicine is challenging and exciting, it is also unpredictable. You never know who is going to walk through the door or if you'll be in control of the situation. Inner-city hospitals are seeing more gang-related emergencies; some emergency rooms have temporarily turned into battle zones, as rival gang members have followed the victims in for treatment.

Emergency medicine can be exhausting work, with the doctor moving in high gear from one crisis to the next. This specialty calls for shift work and on-call rotation, so the hours are far more demanding than with other jobs. Naturally, it's harder to carry on a "normal" home life when you're not there much of the time.

Doctors who've worked in the specialty for a number of years can become cynical. High-stress jobs (where you continually encounter life-and-death situations) sap you of energy and, in some cases, of **idealism**. It's hard not to get disillusioned when you see so much abuse, and despite your intervention, the abuse keeps taking place. It's hard, too, to save someone's life, knowing they're just going to return to the streets and their drinking.

You're constantly exposed to disease and life-threatening conditions like AIDS.

You might spend a good part of your morning reviving a person who's attempted suicide, only to be despised for having brought him back to life.

You face certain ethical dilemmas: how hard do you try to resuscitate someone when you know he's already severely brain damaged? What do you tell the parents of a pregnant fourteen-year-old who think their daughter's sick with the flu? How much effort goes into resuscitating a person dying of AIDS?

If you enjoy working with patients, one of the disadvantages to this specialty is that you never get to find out what happens to them once they leave your hands. You might see a child who's reportedly fallen down the stairs and discover upon examination old injuries and bruises. You suspect abuse, report your suspicions to DHS, and admit the patient to the hospital for continued observation. Days later, you wonder what will happen to him. You stabilize a person who survived a car accident, but with massive injuries. You send him on to surgery, and it's out of your hands. Will he survive? Will he be able to live a normal life again?

It's no fun uncovering abuse—physical or sexual. There are lengthy reports to fill out, parents to confront, and the possibility of testifying in court (if charges are pressed).

As in any medical specialty, you have a lot of paperwork. Because of the ever-present threat of a malpractice suit, you have to be conscientious in your documentation. Sometimes, there seem to be too many patients to see, and no time to write in their charts.

PROFESSIONAL ORGANIZATION
American College of Emergency Physicians
P.O. Box 619911
Dallas, TX 75261-9911

BOARD OF CERTIFICATION
The American Board of Emergency Medicine
200 Woodland Pass
East Lansing, MI 48823

17

Other Medical Opportunities

In this chapter, let's look at some of the other opportunities that exist to practice medicine. In most of the specialties, doctors can combine teaching and research. Some doctors choose to return to the university setting, teaching new students how to be doctors. Usually, the person has practiced for a few years in the community so that he or she has field experience to draw upon.

It's not true that people turn to teaching because they can't do anything better. Teaching is a demanding profession; it requires you to be knowledgable, patient, and a good communicator. It's one thing to be a skilled doctor; it's quite another to be able to impart your knowledge and skill to others. You have to like students in the first place, and you have to be willing to take on all the extra teaching tasks—like grading papers, preparing lectures and exams, meeting with students.

If you discover you possess neither the energy nor the desire to oversee students' work, you might consider offering a workshop on a subject in your specialty. Offering a course at a community college (while still practicing medicine) may convince you whether or not you're cut out for this kind of work.

You can do research in any of the specialties. Dermatologists experiment with new medicines for treatment of skin disorders; neurologists keep looking for that elusive cure for Parkinson's disease or multiple sclerosis; pathologists are currently looking for drugs to combat AIDS. Some doctors enter fellowships to fund their research efforts for a year or two. You can also make a full-time job out of it; researchers work for many government agencies, including the National Institutes of Health.

An administrative job allows you to climb the ladder in your department, practicing the same kind of medicine, but additionally running the department. Running a hospital or an HMO gives you the opportunity to combine your medical knowledge with good business sense. If you're energetic, self-confident, self-starting, and have good communication skills, you might enjoy directing the course of a hospital (or psychiatric facility). Be prepared to deal with the public, though, because administrators have to integrate their hospitals into the community. And realize that it takes more than good medical skills to make a successful hospital administrator; a head for business is just as helpful, if not more so.

Some family physicans (or internists) volunteer to be team doctor for the local high school. If you like sports and have the time, this is a good way to involve yourself in your community. You'll need to be outgoing and energetic to tolerate the pace of this part-time activity. You'll, no doubt, be expected to handle all the athletes' physicals exams, and you'll accompany the team to all the games. Depending on your community, this could be a prestigous job.

Other doctors who practice sports medicine may go on to full-time jobs with professional teams or the Olympic Games. Though, of course, you can't exactly plan for a career as an Olympic physician.

Many surgeons (and anesthesiologists) give a month

103

or so of their time to go to an underdeveloped country and perform surgery on people who need it. Some doctors even take their own equipment with them. Most of these people would never receive surgery if it weren't for these doctors who volunteer their time and skills.

What makes a doctor do something like this? Some do it for the adventure, going to another country and having new experiences. Some who feel that they've been blessed in their lives here, go overseas to give something to others less fortunate. If you're interested in taking a month out of your practice to volunteer your services overseas, you'll find many ads in your medical journals. You're rewarded with adventure, new challenges, comrades who share your values, and more gratitude than you can imagine. And of course, healing those who could never afford the help otherwise, is in itself reward.

Chronicle Guidance Publications has career descriptions of over 600 professions. If you are interested in a medical career that we have not explored here, you can write to them for a complete listing of their job briefs (4 to 5 page descriptions, including educational requirements and job opportunities):

Chronicle Guidance Publications
P.O. Box 1190
66 Aurora St.
Moravia, NY 13118-1190

A $2 fee (plus shipping and handling) is charged for each brief requested.

PART THREE

CONCERNS OF DOCTORS IN MODERN TIMES

18

Ethical Dilemmas in Quality of Life Issues

A doctor's life is not just having the right medical skills to heal a patient. Sometimes the doctor has to decide when to withhold those very skills. In this chapter, let's look at some of the ethical dilemmas facing doctors today. If you're interested in a medical career, you may find yourself confronted with one of these problems. Better consider now whether you have the desire (or courage) to make such decisions.

"Pulling the Plug"
If you're working with terminally ill patients (whether in a hospital or a nursing home), at some point you'll have to look at what you're doing to improve or maintain their quality of life. If all you're doing is prolonging their suffering, resuscitating them again and again to face a painful existence, perhaps you need to sit down with the patient and/or the family and decide when "enough is enough." Ethicists have now declared that DNR (do not resuscitate) orders are morally appropriate because all you're doing is letting nature takes its inevitable course.

107

Unfortunately, our technical knowledge has made it possible to keep patients alive long after they've stopped being able to enjoy that life. As a doctor, you need to decide at what point your intervention is merely delaying death and prolonging your patient's suffering.

If you put a DNR order on a patient's chart, you have to be very certain that the family and/or the patient understand the order. If they are the ones to request such an order, do they understand its implications? If the patient requests not to be resuscitated at any point, is he or she competent to make that decision? (Or was her thinking clouded from depression, for example?) And even if you think she's competent to make the judgment, have you discussed it with her family? Will they protest the decision and fight you in court?

What happens when you're responsible for a newborn whose lungs are far too undeveloped to function properly? Do you still aggressively treat this infant (including full resuscitations), even when you know she won't live past the weekend?

What about "pulling the plug" on patients: taking out the feeding tube or disconnecting the respirator (that wonderful machine that can breathe for us when we can't)? If you remove these life supports, is that the same as "killing" the patient? Is it your job to keep people alive who cannot benefit from life?

Along the same line, if you know that your patient is painfully dying of an inoperable cancer, do you give him antibiotics to cure his pneumonia (or withhold them to speed his death)? Furthermore, is the decision **yours** to make? Does it belong to the patient, the family members (who may want their loved one around at all costs, or who may want him long gone for his estate), or a third party—the hospital ethics committee (who have no relationship with this person)? What if you don't agree with the decision?

approach family members about donating a de-
patient's organs? Is it ethical to push the issue
uctant relatives? What if a patient agreed to
his organs, but upon his death relatives refuse
you to have them? The patient is dead, but
tives are very much alive (and can sue); whose
do you honor? What's your opinion on organ
s, anyway? Should everyone be required to do-
m, since they're of no use once you're dead?
paying people for their body parts be ethical, or
ge untimely deaths?

Y ON JEHOVAH'S WITNESSES

ovah Witnesses' religion does not allow its ad-
to accept blood transfusions. If you are this
surgeon, will you want to operate knowing that
vent of need you won't be able to order a blood
ion? Is it ethical to refuse to operate unless the
agrees to a possible transfusion in an emergency?
ical to ignore the patient's religious principles
him the transfusion anyway?

SK SURGERIES

urgeons agree to operate on patients who have a
ance of surviving surgery, but no chance without
se surgeons give it their best shot, but obviously
re patients than their colleague who is unwilling
on risky candidates. Here's the dilemma: When
keep statistics on surgeons, the ones who are
to take the high-risk cases are going to look
n paper. The figures will show that they have
uccess rates than their colleagues. If the public
ts the statistics to mean that a certain surgeon is
ood as another (who doesn't operate on high-risk
), won't that discourage the braver surgeon from

ACTIVELY ASSISTING SUICIDE

It is one thing to withhold life-prolonging medical technology; it is quite another to actively help a patient
to die. It's easy to dismiss what Dr. Jack Kevorkian
has been doing as the work of a "crazy" man—giving
people the means (prescriptions or knowledge) with
which to commit suicide. Is it really unethical, though,
to help a person leave this life when all that lies ahead is
more pain and suffering?

Dr. Kevorkian, a retired pathologist, first entered the
limelight in 1990 when he helped Janet Adkins to die.
She was diagnosed with Alzheimer's disease, which is
progressively disabling and incurable. Michigan stripped
him of his medical license, but he continued to help
people take their lives. In February 1993 the state
passed a law banning assisted suicide.

Isn't a doctor obligated to save lives, not take them?
Of course, you think, but is it humane to stand by and
watch someone die a slow, agonizing death when you
possess the knowledge (and sometimes the means) to
grant them a speedier death? That is exactly what Dr.
Kevorkian thinks. People get in touch with him when
they want to die and need his help. He says he studies
their medical condition and prognosis; he consults with
their attending physicians regarding the likelihood of
continued deterioration, suffering and/or death, and he
counsels with the individual and family members to
make sure the person is competent to make this decision. It is only after extensive counseling and prep-
aration that Kevorkian agrees to help them die a more
peaceful, dignified death. To Kevorkian, death is not
the enemy; suffering and incapacitation are. He is re-
lieving them of both.

Before you hail Kevorkian's achievements, however,
consider the problem that arises when you put yourself
on a par with God. If you (the doctor) have the right to

assist someone to die, how do I (an ordinary citizen) know you're not going to abuse that right? How do I know that you're not going to decide when *you alone* think someone has outlived his usefulness and encourage him to die? How do I know that you won't be swayed by unethical family members who want to get rid of an ailing relative? What if, at the last moment, a patient decides he really doesn't want to go through with it? Will you honor his change of heart, or will you go ahead anyway? After all, he can't complain when he's gone.

What might happen if a patient could legally opt for a quick, painless death over a more drawn-out, natural death? Would some people choose to die to spare their families the cost of medical treatment? Would some families encourage their suicide for the same reason? Who monitors (and how?) the cases of abuse?

Perhaps you say you'll never have to make such a decision because you don't plan to help anyone die. Well, here's another dilemma that you might encounter: What happens if you (with all your medical expertise) define a course of treatment to a patient, who then refuses your help. Without your treatment, she will likely die. You can't declare her incompetent, because she's mentally sound. In short, you can't make her undergo treatment to save her life. **She has the right to refuse treatment even if it will result in her death**. Will you try to find a family member to overrule her; will you try to get her declared incompetent? Or will you just accept the fact that people have the right not to act in their own best interest?

LIMITED RESOURCES
Part of the problem with our health care system is that we have finite resources. There simply are not enough beds available in the Intensive Care Unit (ICU) of any hospital, and there aren't enough organs available for

transplant. So, how do you go limited resources?

More people survive heart at modern defibrillators and close health may never significantly place where people get the most hospital can provide. How lon depends on his ability to benef treatment and the number of bec a patient in ICU may be moved simply because a more needy p Sending the first patient to a re sion that you've done all you can technology, the patient will prol other ward. Leaving the ICU (would only have prolonged, not i ably will result in earlier death. his bed in the ICU recovers. Wa value than the second? Who det will no longer benefit from int it ever hinge on whether the seemingly more likely to benefit Should the patient or his fami this decision? And if the hospit the decision, are you obligated t

Likewise, who gets the new limited supply—the patient mor it or the one who can actually af

And when we're considering t the top of the list: the man who' to live) or the man with fewer m ensure a better outcome)? Shoul broadcast his need on televisior comes available, or should it re finally made it to the top of the l

And because organs are in sud

docto
cease
with
donat
to all
the re
wishe
donat
nate
Woul
encou

SURG
The
heren
patier
in the
transf
patier
Is it
and g

HIGH-
Some
poor
it. Th
lose n
to tak
peopl
willin
worse
lower
interp
not as
patien

taking on these cases? And should a surgeon agree to operate only if he thinks the outcome will be a positive one? What recourse is left the patient who has no chance to live otherwise?

19

Ethical Dilemmas in Reproductive Issues

ABORTIONS

Hippocrates clearly forbids a doctor to perform an abortion; it's right there in the Hippocratic Oath: ". . . and I will not aid a woman to procure abortion." However, times have changed. Many people believe that women will seek abortions whether they are legal or not; and if that's the case, it is far better for a trained physician to perform the procedure than a back-alley abortionist. Whatever your personal belief, it is still legal in 1993 to perform an abortion. However, if your personal belief does not permit you to perform one yourself, will you still provide women with abortion information?

Suppose, though, you agree that abortion is every woman's right. In these times when pro-life groups are disrupting clinics where doctors perform abortions, are you ready to face such harassment? Are you willing to have your ruputation impugned?

Let's say that abortion is not the issue. As an obstetrician, you have a woman (in her 21st week of pregnancy) whose membranes have just ruptured. If you deliver the baby, he couldn't possibly live at this point. If you don't deliver the baby within 24 to 48 hours, the mother risks an infection that could kill both the baby and herself. What do you do? Delivering the baby would be condemning it to death; doing nothing would be condemning the mother.

Let's say that you do not object to performing abortions. What do you think about using fetal tissue in research? President Clinton has removed the ban on using fetal tissue; previous research has already helped some people recover to some extent from Parkinson's Disease (by transplanting fetal cells into the victim's brain).

Is fetal tissue donation the same as organ donation? Who "owns" the tissue of an aborted fetus? The doctor who performed the abortion, or the woman who was pregnant? And if the woman donates the tissue, does she have any say in who will benefit from it? What would prevent a woman from becoming pregnant intending to abort the fetus and donate fetal tissue to a friend or relative? Could a doctor get rich from selling fetal tissue to scientists for research?

IN-VITRO FERTILIZATION

Because of scientific advances, doctors can create a baby in a test tube (by combining the man's sperm with the woman's egg). But is it ethical? Many couples would never have a child without the doctor's help. If a woman's fallopian tubes are too scarred to permit passage of sperm and egg, how is this woman to get pregnant? If doctors have the ability to induce ovulation, extract the eggs from the ovary, combine them with the man's sperm and implant the fertilized eggs in the woman's womb, can it be wrong?

What if the woman has no uterus, but has perfectly healthy eggs and a husband with perfectly healthy sperm? Since doctors can combine the egg and sperm artificially, why isn't it also acceptable to implant the fertilized eggs into another woman, who can then carry the baby (or babies) to term? Is it ethical to "rent out your uterus"? What happens if the woman carrying this other couple's child decides not to give it up at birth?

Our technological skills have surpassed our wisdom at times. The courts are now grappling with the ethics of surrogate mothers and frozen fertilized eggs. (In one case, a woman is suing her ex-husband for "custody of the embryos." He does not want her to have the embryos implanted; he doesn't want offspring to support now that they're divorced. The woman wants to use the embryos to get pregnant. To whom do these embryos belong?)

Some people even fight over frozen sperm deposits. One man (who committed suicide) had donated his sperm so that his girlfriend could get inseminated with it after he died. His family now won't let this woman have access to his sperm deposit; they question his intention (as well as his sanity) when he made this promise. The woman believes they simply don't want any more heirs to his estate. . . . In the meantime, who gets control of the sperm?

A woman, past menopause, gave birth in 1992. A younger woman had donated her egg (which was then fertilized with the sperm of the older woman's husband and was implanted into the postmenopausal woman). Which now means that women over the age of fifty can continue having babies (with a donor's help). How will these older mothers affect the family of the future?

As our technical knowledge increases, we face more confusing ethical dilemmas in the medical profession. Just because you possess these skills doesn't mean it's always right to use them. How do you weigh the benefits against the problems these could create? Does MONEY ever have anything to do with it?

Sex and Patients

The doctor/patient relationship is one of power/vulner-ability. The patient comes to you expecting help. It's not unusual for a patient to "fall in love" with his or her doctor. You (the doctor) are caring and helping the patient to feel better. Gratitude sometimes makes a person do things she wouldn't do under other circum-stances. Likewise, because patients are naked (some-times only figuratively speaking), appreciative, and trusting, they may tempt you to stretch the boundaries of your relationship. Sex with a patient is *always* unethi-cal. (Which doesn't mean it's never done.)

To understand why the sexual boundaries are neces-sary, you have to consider the doctor/patient relation-ship like the adult/child's. The patient comes to you for help with a medical or psychiatric problem. To turn the visit into a sexual opportunity (or to respond to her overtures) would be to confuse the issue. Sex is engaged in by equals. The patient, like the child, is in a vulner-able position; she is not your equal in this situation. Were you to be known for giving in to temptation, how would other patients trust you to respect their boundaries? Most patients expect you to behave profes-sionally; sometimes, their sexual advances are only bold attempts to change the focus of the visit (particularly in psychiatric sessions). Making use of transference issues doesn't mean breaching sexual boundaries. For the pa-tient's peace of mind, and yours, remember that you can, **and should**, lose your license for having sex with a patient.

20

The Changing Climate of Medicine

THE COST OF TREATMENT

America and South Africa are the only modern countries that do not consider health care a universal right. That means that only persons with proper medical insurance receive the best care. Those able to comply with governmental regulations get Medicare and Medicaid, but will they get the same opportunities (and care) as the wealthier patient? Who will treat the patients who can't pay? What happens when the type of medical assistance offered (surgery, diagnostic tests, experimental drugs) depends on the person's ability to pay?

Critically ill cancer patients can now have their lives extended (but not necessarily improved) with costly medical care. Some may live for two extra years, at a staggering cost of $82,000 to $189,340 (for bone marrow transplants and chemotherapy, etc.). Is it fair to spend this amount of money on a person whose condition will not substantially improve? Is it fair that only **some** people can afford this kind of expense? But what of the alternatives? What would socialized medicine do to the current practice of medicine? Would patients still be

118

shortchanged (as many doctors predict) with less personal attention?

Many doctors are already complaining about the paperwork involved in getting reimbursement from insurance companies, not to mention the difficulty getting approval to hospitalize their patients for a sufficient length of time. They believe that third parties (insurance companies) have diminished the doctor's role by regulating how long he or she can hospitalize a patient and by determining how much he can be reimbursed for his treatment. Wouldn't more government regulation only increase the role of third parties in the practice of medicine? And just how do they determine what a patient needs when they have no intimate knowledge of that patient's condition?

Health Maintenance Organization

One way doctors are combatting this problem is banding together to offer a complete range of services to persons insured through their employers. People get all their health needs met in one place, at reduced cost—as long as they consult the doctors at this HMO. Doctors are usually encouraged to consider the least costly medical interventions. They may end up receiving the money (in the form of a bonus) that was saved by not ordering expensive tests, for example. Some doctors argue that they're only practicing good medicine—not recommending any more diagnostic procedures than necessary. But are they shortchanging the patients in the interest of the profit margin? These are the questions that bother the public today. In an HMO, is a doctor as free to use his medical knowledge and skills as he would be in private practice?

What if you (as a patient in an HMO) want a particular surgeon (with a better reputation) to perform your operation, but you'd have to pay him out of your own

119

pocket. Is it fair that you can't have the "best" possible surgeon because he's not in the HMO's employ? Is it fair that the only way to retain him is to find the money yourself? To which surgeon will the first doctor refer you: the one in his group or the one he knows is more skilled at your particular operation?

Bill Collecting and "The Good Doctor" Image

People want to see you as the good doctor who is out there practicing, sometimes out of the goodness of his heart. What do you suppose happens to that benevolent image when you send the collection agents after them for not paying their bill? It may not represent much of an ethical dilemma to you, since your family needs to live, too, but wrangling payment out of patients does represent an unpleasant part of the job.

The Threat of Malpractice Suits

American society is increasingly litigious, especially over doctors. While other human beings are entitled to their mistakes, doctors appear not to be—perhaps because medical errors can be fatal. So it's only common sense that you insure yourself against the possibility of being sued.

How does the threat of a malpractice suit affect your practice of medicine? For one thing, the high cost of insurance may turn you away from the higher-risk specialties, like obstetrics. For another thing, you'll probably order more (expensive) tests to confirm your diagnosis. It may make you reluctant to take on risky cases or to take any risks with your patients.

What if you know that a particular doctor is **not** practicing good medicine? Should you report him to the state licensing board? Should you testify against him? How might testifying affect your own practice? Most doctors depend on their colleagues for referrals; if doctors fear that you're looking over their shoulders at how they practice medicine, might they not stop referring patients to you? How long can you last in a community that ignores (or worse, despises) you?

On the other hand, if you know that a doctor is doing something that's either dangerous or unethical, does failure to speak up make you an accomplice? The public (in these cases) is expecting someone in your situation to protect them. Do you owe them anything?

EXPOSURE TO AIDS

Doctors have always risked exposure to certain contagious diseases; most diseases and infections have cures. AIDS (acquired immunodeficiency syndrome) does not. Since the HIV human immunodeficiency virus is passed in body fluids, the doctor runs some risk of contamination whenever he or she sticks a needle into a patient who has AIDS. Surgeons face a greater risk, since they routinely cut into a patient. How will AIDS affect the practice of medicine? Naturally, until a cure (or a vaccine) is developed, doctors are going to approach their patients with more caution, wearing gloves and masks for even routine procedures. Is it ethical, let alone legal, to require any of your patients to be tested for AIDS if they are to undergo invasive procedures?

While doctors may not deny treatment to people simply because they fear the AIDS virus, will some be less aggressive in their treatment of AIDS patients? How quickly will they respond to a psychotic patient known to have AIDS? Will they view every drug abuser or homosexual as someone harboring the virus? Will they, then, offer the same quality of care they offer others?

And what about confidentiality? If you know a person has tested positive to HIV, and you know his previous partners, are you obligated to breach confidentiality (assuming he won't tell them)? If you are a psychiatrist providing marital therapy to a couple, and you know the man is having an affair (which subjects his wife to venereal disease and AIDS), how do you bring the issue out into the open?

Being a doctor today means possessing knowledge and skills you may not always get to use. Bear in mind that the ethical doctor knows not only her own limitations, but the limitations of her profession.

If you decide to embark on a medical career, we wish you enough energy, compassion, and integrity to last you a lifetime.

Appendix
U.S. Medical Schools

Alabama
University of Alabama School of Medicine
Birmingham, AL 35294

University of South Alabama College of Medicine
Mobile, AL 36688

Arizona
University of Arizona College of Medicine
Tucson, AZ 85724

Arkansas
University of Arkansas College of Medicine
Little Rock, AR 77205

California
Loma Linda University School of Medicine
Loma Linda, CA 92350

Stanford University School of Medicine
Stanford, CA 94305

University of California, Davis, School of Medicine
Davis, CA 95616

Connecticut
Yale University School of Medicine
New Haven, CT 06510

District of Columbia
Georgetown University School of Medicine
Washington, DC 20007

George Washington University
School of Medicine and Health Sciences
Washington DC 20037

Howard University College of Medicine
Washington DC 20059

Florida
University of Florida College of Medicine
Gainesville, FL 32610

University of Miami School of Medicine
Miami, FL 33101

University of South Florida College of Medicine
Tampa, FL 33612

Georgia
Emory University School of Medicine
Atlanta, GA 30322

Medical College of Georgia
Augusta, GA 30912

Mercer University School of Medicine
Macon, GA 31207

Morehouse School of Medicine
Atlanta, GA 30314

Hawaii
University of Hawaii
John A. Burns School of Medicine
Honolulu, HI 96822

Illinois
Loyola University of Chicago
Stritch School of Medicine
Maywood, IL 60153

Northwestern University Medical School
Chicago, IL 60611

Rush Medical College
Chicago, IL 60612

Southern Illinois University School of Medicine
Springfield, IL 62708

University of Chicago Pritzker School of Medicine
Chicago, IL 60637

University of Health Sciences
The Chicago Medical School
North Chicago, IL 60064

University of Illinois College of Medicine
Chicago, IL 60612

Indiana
Indiana University School of Medicine
Indianapolis, IN 46223

Iowa
University of Iowa College of Medicine
Iowa City, IA 52242

Kansas
University of Kansas School of Medicine
Kansas City, KA 66103

Kentucky
University of Kentucky College of Medicine
Lexington, KY 40536

University of Louisville School of Medicine
Louisville, KY 40292

Louisiana
Louisiana State University School of Medicine in
New Orleans
New Orleans, LA 70112

Louisiana State University School of Medicine in
Shreveport
Shreveport, LA 71130

Tulane University School of Medicine
New Orleans, LA 70112

Maryland
The Johns Hopkins University School of Medicine
Baltimore, MD 21205

Uniformed Services University of the Health
Sciences
F. Edward Hebert School of Medicine
Bethesda, MD 20014

University of Maryland School of Medicine
Baltimore, MD 21201

Massachusetts
Boston University School of Medicine
Boston, MA 02118

Harvard Medical School
Boston, MA 02115

Tufts University School of Medicine
Boston, MA 02111

University of Massachusetts Medical School
Worcester, MA 01605

Michigan
Michigan State University College of Human Medicine
East Lansing, MI 48824

University of Michigan Medical School
Ann Arbor, MI 48109

Wayne State University School of Medicine
Detroit, MI 48201

Minnesota
Mayo Medical School
Rochester, MN 55905

University of Minnesota Duluth School of Medicine
Duluth, MN 55812

University of Minnesota Medical School
Minneapolis, MN 55455

Mississippi
University of Mississippi School of Medicine
Jackson, MS 39216

Missouri
Saint Louis University School of Medicine
St. Louis, MO 63104

University of Missouri Columbia School of Medicine
Columbia, MO 65212

University of Missouri Kansas City School of Medicine
Kansas City, MO 64108

Washington University Medical School
St. Louis, MO 63110

Nebraska
Creighton University School of Medicine
Omaha, NE 68178

University of Nebraska College of Medicine
Omaha, NE 68105

Nevada
University of Nevada School of Medicine
Reno, NV 89557

New Hampshire
Dartmouth Medical School
Hanover, NH 03756

New Jersey
University of Medicine and Dentistry of New Jersey—
New Jersey Medical School
Newark, NJ 07103

University of Medicine and Dentistry—Robert Wood
Johnson Medical School
Piscataway, NJ 08854

New Mexico
University of New Mexico School of Medicine
Albuquerque, NM 87131

New York
Albany Medical College of Union University
Albany, NY 12208

Albert Einstein College of Medicine of Yeshiva
  University
New York, NY 10461

Columbia University College of Physicians and Surgeons
New York, NY 10032

Cornell University Medical College
New York, NY 10021

Mount Sinai School of Medicine of the City University
  of New York
New York, NY 10029

New York Medical College
Valhalla, NY 10595

New York University School of Medicine
New York, NY 10016

State University of New York Health Science Center at
  Brooklyn
Brooklyn, NY 11203

State University of New York at Buffalo School of
  Medicine
Buffalo, NY 14214

State University of New York at Stony Brook School of
Medicine
Stony Brook, NY 11794

State University of New York Health Science Center at
Syracuse
Syracuse, NY 13210

University of Rochester School of Medicine and
Dentistry
Rochester, NY 14642

North Carolina
Bowman Gray School of Medicine of Wake Forest
University
Winston-Salem, NC 27103

Duke University School of Medicine
Durham, NC 27710

East Carolina University School of Medicine
Greenville, NC 27834

University of North Carolina at Chapel Hill School of
Medicine
Chapel Hill, NC 27514

North Dakota
University of North Dakota School of Medicine
Grand Forks, ND 58202

Ohio
Case Western Reserve University School of Medicine
Cleveland, OH 44106

Medical College of Ohio at Toledo
Toledo, OH 43699

Northeastern Ohio Universities College of Medicine
Rootstown, OH 44272

Ohio State University College of Medicine
Columbus, OH 43210

University of Cincinnati College of Medicine
Cincinnati, OH 45267

Wright State University School of Medicine
Dayton, OH 45401

Oklahoma
University of Oklahoma College of Medicine
Oklahoma City, OK 73190

Oregon
Oregon Health Sciences University School of Medicine
Portland, OR 97201

Pennsylvania
Hahnemann University School of Medicine
Philadelphia, PA 19102

Jefferson Medical College of Thomas Jefferson
University
Philadelphia, PA 19107

Medical College of Pennsylvania
Philadelphia, PA 19129

Pennsylvania State University College of Medicine
Hershey, PA 17033

Temple University School of Medicine
Philadelphia, PA 19140

University of Pennsylvania School of Medicine
Philadelphia, PA 19104

University of Pittsburgh School of Medicine
Pittsburgh, PA 15261

Puerto Rico
Ponce School of Medicine
Ponce, PR 00732

Universidad Central del Caribe Escuela de Medicina
Cayey, PR 00633

University of Puerto Rico School of Medicine
San Juan, PR 00936

Rhode Island
Brown University Program in Medicine
Providence, RI 02912

South Carolina
Medical University of South Carolina College of
    Medicine
Charleston, SC 29425

University of South Carolina School of Medicine
Columbia, SC 29208

South Dakota
University of South Dakota School of Medicine
Vermillion, SD 57069

Tennessee
East Tennessee State University James H. Dishner
College of Medicine
Johnson City, TN 37614

Meharry Medical College School of Medicine
Nashville, TN 37208

University of Tennessee College of Medicine
Memphis, TN 38163

Vanderbilt University School of Medicine
Nashville, TN 37232

Texas
Baylor College of Medicine
Houston, TX 77030

Texas A & M University College of Medicine
College Station, TX 77843

Texas Tech University Health Sciences Center School
of Medicine
Lubbock, TX 79430

University of Texas Medical Branch at Galveston
Galveston, TX 77550

University of Texas Medical School at Houston
Houston, TX 77225

University of Texas Medical School at San Antonio
San Antonio, TX 78284

University of Texas Southwestern Medical Center at Dallas School of Medicine
Dallas, TX 75235

Utah
University of Utah School of Medicine
Salt Lake City, UT 84132

Vermont
University of Vermont College of Medicine
Burlington, VT 05405

Virginia
Eastern Virginia Medical School
Norfolk, VA 23501

University of Virginia School of Medicine
Charlottesville, VA 22908

Virginia Commonwealth University Medical College of Virginia
Richmond, VA 23298

Washington
University of Washington School of Medicine
Seattle, WA 98195

West Virginia
Marshall University School of Medicine
Huntington, WV 25701

West Virginia University School of Medicine
Morgantown, WV 26506

Wisconsin
Medical College of Wisconsin
Milwaukee, WI 53226

University of Wisconsin Medical School
Madison, WI 53706

For Further Reading

Aaseng, Nathan. *The Inventors*. Minneapolis: Lerner Publications Co. 1988.

Ablow, Keith Russell. *Medical School*. New York: St. Martin's Press, 1990.

Brown, Jordan. *Elizabeth Blackwell*. New York: Chelsea House Publishers, 1989.

Dubler, Nancy, and Nimmons, David. *Ethics on Call*. New York: Harmony Books, 1992.

Fekete, Irene, and Ward, Peter Dorrington. *Disease and Medicine*. New York: Facts on File Publications, 1985.

Klass, Perri, *Baby Doctor*. New York: Random House, 1992.

Marion, Robert. *The Intern Blues*. New York: Fawcett Crest, 1989.

Nuland, Sherwin. *Doctors*. New York: Alfred A. Knopf, 1988.

Pekkanen, John. *MD Doctors Talk About Themselves*. New York: Dell Publishing, 1988.

Rabinowitz, Peter MacGarr. *Talking Medicine*. New York: W.W. Norton & Co., 1981.

Rainer, J. Kenyon. *First Do No Harm*. New York: Villard Books, 1987.

Seager, Stephen, M.D. *Psych Ward*. New York: G.P. Putnam's Sons, 1991.

Shorter, Edward. *The Health Century*. New York: Doubleday, 1987.

Turvey, Peter. *Timelines Inventions: Inventors and Ingenious Ideas*. New York: Franklin Watts, 1992.

Wilson, Josleen. *The American Society of Plastic and*

Reconstructive Surgeons' Guide to Cosmetic Surgery. New York: Simon & Schuster, 1992.

Ziegler, Edward. *Emergency Doctor.* New York: Ballantine Books, 1987.

Index

transplant, organ, 11, 50, 54,
110–112
treatment
costs of, 118–121
discontinuing, 17, 47
patient's refusal of, 110

U
ultrasound, 68, 80, 82
urologist, 37, 49, 50, 52

V
Vesalius, Andreas, 4, 5
volunteering, physicians, 103–
104

W
Wells, Horace, 5
women
first entering medicine, 6–7
liking for, by obstetrician, 70
in medical school, 25
in obstetrics, 71
in pathology, 85, 87
in pediatrics, 76

X
x-ray, 10, 38, 41, 44, 45, 47, 61,
79–81